Dorling Kindersley

VISUAL TIMELINE OF

Transportation

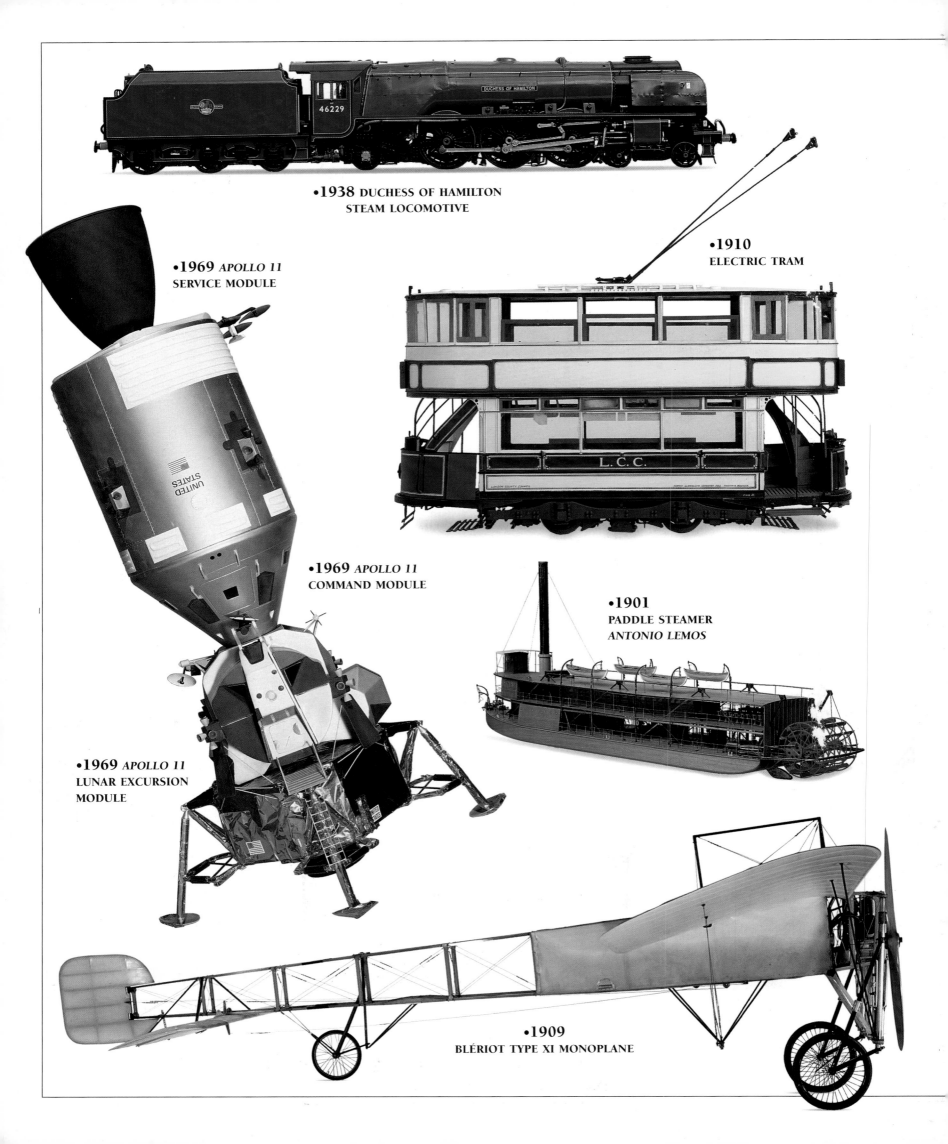

•**1938** DUCHESS OF HAMILTON
STEAM LOCOMOTIVE

•**1910**
ELECTRIC TRAM

•**1969** *APOLLO 11*
SERVICE MODULE

•**1969** *APOLLO 11*
COMMAND MODULE

•**1901**
PADDLE STEAMER
ANTONIO LEMOS

•**1969** *APOLLO 11*
LUNAR EXCURSION
MODULE

•**1909**
BLÉRIOT TYPE XI MONOPLANE

Dorling Kindersley
VISUAL TIMELINE OF
Transportation

ANTHONY WILSON

•1988 FERRARI TESTAROSSA

c.**750**
CHINESE BUFFALO CART

•**1939**
BISMARCK
BATTLESHIP

•**1784**
MONTGOLFIER BROTHERS'
FLESSELLES HOT-AIR BALLOON

DORLING KINDERSLEY   DEC - - 1996
LONDON • NEW YORK • STUTTGART

A DORLING KINDERSLEY BOOK

Project Editor Stephen Setford
Art Editor Lester Cheeseman
Managing Editor Helen Parker
Managing Art Editor Peter Bailey
U.S. Editor Camela Decaire
Picture Research Anna Lord
Editorial Researcher Robert Graham
Production Louise Barratt & Ruth Cobb
Editorial Consultant Eryl Davies

First American Edition, 1995
2 4 6 8 10 9 7 5 3 1

Published in the United States by
Dorling Kindersley Publishing, Inc., 95 Madison Avenue,
New York, New York 10016

Library of Congress Cataloging-in-Publication Data

Wilson, Anthony
    Dorling Kindersley visual timeline of transportation /
Anthony Wilson. – 1st American ed.
    p.   cm.
    Includes index
    ISBN 1-56458-880-7
    1. Transportation-History. I. Title.
TA1015.W55   1995   94-48714
629.04-dc20   CIP

Reproduced by Colourscan, Singapore

Printed and bound in Italy by
A. Mondadori Editore, Verona

Contents

Foreword

THE STORY OF TRANSPORTATION is the story of our ingenuity in devising new ways of moving people and goods from place to place. Transportation has been essential to human life for thousands of years: simple carts and boats were as vital to the farming and fishing communities of the past as automobiles, trains, buses, and airplanes are to us today. Because transportation affects our day-to-day lives so profoundly, much of this *Visual Timeline* focuses on the everyday means of transportation that ordinary people have used and relied upon over the centuries.

Some of the vehicles, crafts, and vessels in this book are not typical, but are included because they carried people on famous voyages of exploration – to distant parts of the world, to the depths of the oceans, and even to the Moon. Others have been chosen to show how transportation has been adapted for an enormous variety of specialized uses, from battleships and bombers to wage war, to surfboards and roller skates for sports and leisure activities.

Also well represented here are "famous firsts" – innovations that represent a significant step forward in the history of transportation. For any such innovation to be widely adopted, it must first pass several tests: does it work well and reliably, and meet a real need? Is its technology appropriate for the people who will use it, so that they can service and maintain it? Above all, is it cheap enough for plenty of people to afford? In the following pages, you will find some ideas – such as the penny farthing bicycle and the Concorde – that failed these tests, as well as many more that were outstandingly successful. Among the "milestones" listed in this book are many of the developments in basic technology – new materials, fuels, and engines, for example – that gave rise to improvements in transportation and its infrastructure, such as new bridges, tunnels, roads, and railroad tracks.

I hope that the *Dorling Kindersley Visual Timeline of Transportation* will give insight into a vital area of our lives that we often take for granted, as well as give a flavor of what is to come. If the future of transportation is as varied and as exciting as its past, then we have a lot to look forward to.

Anthony Wilson

Anthony Wilson

10,000 BC–AD 1779
Traveling at nature's pace

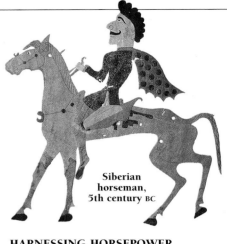

Siberian horseman, 5th century BC

From the time the first humans appeared, half a million years ago, right up to the early 20th century AD, most people lived their lives without ever traveling more than a few miles from where they were born. When they did travel, most of their journeys were made on foot. Even today, the majority of the world's people do not have cars or even bicycles, and seldom ride a bus or train. However, throughout history new methods of transportation have had a dramatic influence on the world in which we live. In the period before 2000 BC, there were three particularly important innovations: the hollowed-out boat, the wheeled cart, and horse riding. Together, they shaped the pattern of transportation up to the late 18th century AD, and their influence is still felt today.

Shoeing horses in northern India, c.AD 1600

The birth of the boat

People probably first took to the water on logs or flat rafts made of small branches tied together. These objects float naturally, but they sink if too much weight is loaded aboard. The first "boat-shaped" boats were made by hollowing out tree trunks. The shape of a hollowed-out boat enables it to carry much more weight than a solid log or raft. By 2500 BC, the Egyptians were building ships from small wooden planks and equipping them with sails.

HARNESSING HORSEPOWER

The horse has played a crucial role in transportation through the ages because it is a fast, strong, hardy animal. Just as cars are made in a variety of shapes and sizes, so people have bred many types of horses, with different qualities to suit different needs. Some were bred to be powerful draft or pack animals, while others were bred for their speed and stamina. The invention of horseshoes enabled horses to travel over more difficult terrain.

Bronze model of a Roman racing chariot, 2nd century AD

The chariots were light for maximum speed, and sometimes very ornate.

During their racing years, champion stallions were used for breeding.

Spoked wheels

THE CHANGING WORLD: 10,000 BC–AD 1799

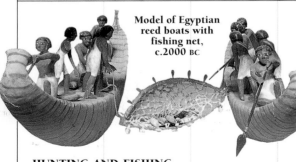

Model of Egyptian reed boats with fishing net, c.2000 BC

HUNTING AND FISHING

The earliest people were wanderers, living in small groups and traveling on foot from place to place in search of food. They lived by hunting wild animals, by fishing, and by picking berries and other food from plants. They had to devise ways of dragging or carrying what they had caught so that they could take it back to share with the rest of their group. They also found that by venturing onto water on simple rafts and floats, they were able to catch more fish.

FARMING

About 10,000 years ago, people began to plant crops. These early farmers no longer needed to roam and hunt and were able to settle in one place for many years. As villages grew into towns, transportation was needed to bring food from the countryside. Animals were reared for food, but they were also used to carry farm produce on their backs and to pull carts and plows. People even learned to ride some species, such as the horse and the elephant.

Chinese model of an ox-drawn plow

The trader and traveler Marco Polo on the Silk Road

MERCHANTS AND TRADERS

Eventually, some people became merchants and traders, buying and selling things that other people needed. They used materials such as salt, animal skins, or pieces of gold and silver in the same way we use money today. Eventually, trade routes thousands of miles long were established, such as the Silk Road, which ran from China to Persia. Each merchant traveled a few hundred miles and then exchanged his goods with the next merchant on the route.

FIGHTING

When communities grew, so did their squabbles. Family arguments turned into tribal battles and then into wars between rival rulers and nations. Transportation was essential to warfare. Armies marched on foot, but needed wagons to carry supplies. Chariots were used to impress and overwhelm the enemy. Warriors on horseback were faster than foot soldiers and had a better vantage point from which to fight. Later, specialized ships were developed for battles at sea.

Mounted archer, 5th century BC

Over the years, two main types of ships developed: sleek warships powered by teams of rowers, and more rounded cargo vessels powered by sail. Ships continued to grow larger, faster, and more versatile, until, by the 15th and 16th centuries AD, European explorers such as Christopher Columbus and Ferdinand Magellan were venturing to distant parts of the world in their three-masted "square-riggers."

The chariot pole is topped by a decorative ram's head.

Horses, wheels, and carts

People first learned to ride horseback about 4,000 years ago. For anyone who could afford it, a horse provided high-speed personal transportation. It also proved invaluable as a "beast of burden" for carrying loads, and as a draft animal for pulling carts and other vehicles. The earliest carts were unwieldy, and their solid wooden wheels needed a good surface to run on. By 2000 BC, carpenters had learned to build wheels with spokes, which were larger and lighter and ran better over uneven ground. Over the next 4,000 years, the cart was adapted into a wide variety of chariots, wagons, coaches, and carriages.

By the late 18th century AD, horse-drawn stagecoaches were rattling through the towns and cities of several countries, and international trade relied on splendid sailing ships that plied the world's oceans. But transportation still depended entirely on animal or wind power, and ships and land vehicles were still built from wood and other natural materials, with only a little metal where it was essential. All this was to change in the years ahead.

TRANSPORTATION TECHNOLOGY

BEATING FRICTION
The wheel is the greatest human victory in the battle against friction, the dragging force that makes it hard to slide a heavy object over a rough surface. When a heavy load is moved on wheels, the part of the wheel that touches the ground does not slide. It rolls, so there is very little friction. Instead, there is some friction where the revolving axle rubs against its mount. People soon learned to reduce this friction by putting a leather sleeve between the moving surfaces, and by using greasy animal fat as a lubricant, another important antifriction device.

Chinese wheelbarrow

The longer the handles of a wheelbarrow, the less force is needed to lift the load.

Friction at the axle is reduced by lubrication.

No sliding occurs where the wheel touches the ground.

STAYING AFLOAT
If you push an empty bottle down into a pool of water, you can feel the water pushing up against you. The water around the bottle presses on it and holds it up. The ancient Greek scientist Archimedes discovered that the more water an object displaces, or pushes out of the way, the more strongly it is held up by the water around it. A hollowed-out boat is not only light in itself, but can also carry a heavy cargo since its shape allows it to displace a lot of water without submerging. And because it is hollow, it can even be made of material such as iron, which does not normally float.

The hollow shape makes the boat displace a large amount of water.

North American Indian birch bark canoe

Water presses on the boat to hold it up.

FINDING THE WAY
The first ocean sailors kept close to familiar shores. To help them navigate, they noted the direction of the Sun as it rose and set, the position of the stars at night, and which way the wind was blowing. Later, instruments such as the astrolabe, which measures the height of the Sun or stars above the horizon, were developed. By about AD 1000, some sailors were navigating using simple magnetic compasses.

Astrolabe, AD 1585

EXPLORING THE WORLD
Throughout history, some people have ventured far from home to find out about the wider world. Others often followed and settled in the places they had visited. Sailors from ancient Greece explored the European and African coasts, setting up colonies. European travelers later reached and settled in the lands now called Australia and America. Ships such as the *Mayflower*, which carried English settlers to America, today seem very small and fragile for such difficult voyages.

Model of the *Mayflower*, AD 1620

Roman road at Pompeii, Italy

EMPIRES AND ROADS
As nations quarreled, rulers invaded and conquered neighboring countries, sometimes creating huge empires. They included the empires of Egypt, Persia, and Rome, and the Mayas of Central America. To rule such large areas, networks of roads were set up so that messengers on horseback could bring news from distant parts in just a few days. Roads also enabled armies to move quickly to trouble spots, and made trade within an empire much easier.

CANALS FOR TRADE
The easiest way to move goods from one place to another was often by boat. Where there was no suitable river, a channel was dug and filled with water to make a canal along which barges could be towed by people or animals. The Egyptians built their first canal more than 4,000 years ago, while the Chinese started work on their Grand Canal in about 500 BC. Canals did not become important trade routes in Europe until medieval times.

Painting of the Grand Canal, China, 18th century AD

10,000 BC

5000 BC

10,000 BC	9000 BC	8000 BC	7000 BC	6000 BC	5000 BC	4600 BC	4200 BC	3800 BC

LAND

Before 10,000 BC TRAVELING ON FOOT

For early people, the only way to travel over land was on foot. Only young children and the sick or injured would get a ride, carried by stronger members of the group. A heavy load, such as a large animal caught for food, would have to be dragged along the ground, or carried on a person's back. A very heavy animal might be slung from a wooden pole, so that its weight could be shared by several people.

Stone Age hunter carrying his kill

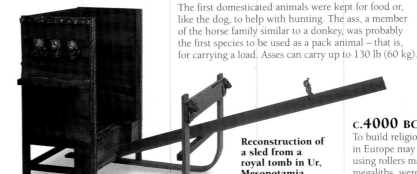

Reconstruction of a sled from a royal tomb in Ur, Mesopotamia, c.2700–2400 BC

Runner

c.5000 BC SLEDS

As an alternative to carrying heavy objects, people learned to drag them along on pieces of animal skin or tree bark. From this, they developed the wooden sled. In Mesopotamia (now part of Iraq), large sleds were used for moving statues or blocks of stone. Smaller ones may have been used by royalty as a kind of chariot. Adding skilike runners beneath the sled reduced friction with the ground, making it easier to pull. *See* VIKING SLED c.AD 850.

c.5000 BC PACK ANIMALS

The first domesticated animals were kept for food or, like the dog, to help with hunting. The ass, a member of the horse family similar to a donkey, was probably the first species to be used as a pack animal – that is, for carrying a load. Asses can carry up to 130 lb (60 kg).

Egyptian procession, showing tame ass as pack animal

c.4000 BC WOODEN ROLLERS

To build religious and astronomical monuments, people in Europe may have moved huge stone building blocks using rollers made from tree trunks. The stones, called megaliths, were first transported from quarries by boat. Rollers were then placed beneath them and they were hauled overland to the building site.

Moving a megalith using wooden rollers

WATER

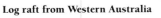

Log raft from Western Australia

c.10,000 BC LOGS AND RAFTS

The first water transportation was probably simply a floating log or tree trunk. Later, people learned to lay branches, or bundles of reeds, side by side and bind them together to make a raft. The raft was controlled by paddling with arms and legs, but people soon found that a flat piece of wood makes a better paddle. To carry more weight, floats were attached around the edge of the raft.

Assyrian carving of man fishing astride an inflated animal skin

c.10,000 BC ANIMAL-SKIN FLOATS

To keep themselves – and their rafts – afloat, people learned how to take the skin of an animal, stitch up the holes, and blow it up like an air cushion. To cross a deep river, they lay across the inflated skin and paddled. Large pots and gourds were also used as floats.

c.7000 BC DUGOUTS

Dugouts – the first real boats – were made by burning the wood from inside one half of a split tree trunk or gouging it out with stone tools. A hollowed-out boat can carry more weight than a raft and is easier to steer. Other early boats were made from strips of tree bark. *See* BARK CANOE AD 1770.

Making a dugout

c.5000 BC SKIN BOATS

Since early times, animal skins have been used as waterproof coverings for boats. The skins were sewn together and stretched over a frame of wooden branches or basketwork. Later basket-boats, such as round quffas and coracles, were waterproofed with pitch – a black material obtained from tar. Quffas, used on the Euphrates River in Babylon more than 2,000 years ago, can still be seen today.

Pitch-covered quffa from Iran

Steering oar

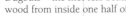

c.3100 BC SAILBOAT *Egypt*

The first sailboats were probably made by the ancient Egyptians. They found that with a square sail, the power of the wind could be harnessed on journeys up the Nile River, where the wind usually blows in the upstream direction. On the return trip downstream, the boat was either paddled or allowed to drift along with the current, steered by a long oar at the back.

The boat is steered from the back, or stern.

Model of an Egyptian sailboat, c.1800 BC

The boat's owner sits beneath an ox-hide canopy.

MILESTONES

10,000–5001 BC

•**10,000 BC** Hunter-gatherer people from Asia spread into North America through Alaska. Eventually, they will spread as far down as the tip of South America, but their rate of progress is slow – only about 10 miles (16 km) a year.

•**10,000 BC** The wolf is the first wild animal to be tamed, or domesticated, becoming the dog. Later, dogs will be used to pull sleds and carts.

•**8000 BC** A paddle found at Star Carr in Yorkshire, England, is the earliest archaeological evidence of water transportation, showing that people living beside a lake there are using boats.

•**8000 BC** People from mainland Greece travel 75 miles (120 km) by sea to the island of Melos to gather obsidian, a glassy stone used to make cutting tools. This is the earliest known long-distance sea voyage.

•**7500 BC** Farming begins in southwestern Asia. To transport their crops, farmers will need carts or sleds, and tamed animals to pull them.

•**6000 BC** Boats are in use for deep-sea fishing off the coasts of Scotland and Sweden in northern Europe.

Reconstruction of early plank wheel

5000–3001 BC

•**5000 BC** Sleds are used to move people and goods over snow, sand, and grassland.

•**5000 BC** Pack animals such as asses are used to carry loads. Other early pack animals are donkeys, camels and elephants in Asia, and llamas in South America.

•**4500 BC** Horses are tamed for the first time, either in the grasslands, or steppes, of the Ukraine, or in what is now Turkey or Iran. They are later used as pack animals.

•**3500 BC** Wheeled vehicles are in use in Mesopotamia. The first one may have been a sled to which four wheels were added.

•**3500 BC** Roads are built in Mesopotamia to help traders move between villages, towns, and cities. Simple bridges of stone slabs help people cross streams.

•**3100 BC** Ships with sails made from bundles of papyrus, a tall, reedlike plant, appear on the Nile River.

3000 BC

2000 BC

3000 BC	2800 BC	2600 BC	2400 BC	2200 BC	2000 BC	1800 BC	1600 BC	1400 BC	1200 BC

c.3000 BC HORSE RIDING

In ancient times, horses roamed wild in many parts of the world. One of the most important developments in the history of transportation came when people first learned to ride horseback – probably about 5,000 years ago. Horses were used for going on journeys, for hunting, and in warfare. Later, the harness was developed to give the rider greater control. It consisted of a bridle (straps fitting around the head) and bit (a metal piece in the mouth).

The ropes supporting the mast and sail are called rigging.

The sail hangs from a wooden beam called a yard.

Armored breastplate

Assyrian warrior riding horse with harness, 7th century BC

c.2400 BC COVERED WAGON *Syria*

The first carts and wagons had many uses. Some belonged to royalty, others to ordinary people called nomads who had no fixed homes and lived in covered wagons or in tents. Traders also used covered wagons, similar to this small pottery model, to transport goods they had made for selling as they moved from town to town.

Pottery model of covered wagon, Syria, c.2500–2300 BC

c.2500 BC FOUR-WHEELED CHARIOT *Mesopotamia*

The first wheeled vehicles may have been made in about 3500 BC by the Sumerian people of Mesopotamia. The earliest chariots probably had four wheels, and were pulled by pairs of animals such as onagers, smaller relations of wild horses. The wheels were made of shaped wooden planks, joined by wooden crosspieces.

Tutankhamen's war chariot, c.1340 BC

c.1340 BC TWO-WHEELED CHARIOT *Egypt*

Lightweight, two-wheeled chariots may have originated in Sumeria around 2500 BC. Pulled by horses, they were fast and easy to maneuver, making them useful in warfare for a surprise attack against foot soldiers. Later Egyptian chariots, such as King Tutankhamen's, had spoked wheels, which are much lighter than solid wheels made from wooden planks. War chariots usually carried two people, one to drive the chariot, and the other to fight.

Four-wheeled Sumerian war chariot, c.2500 BC

c.2600 BC ROYAL BARGE *Egypt*

Some Egyptian ships, such as the magnificent barge made for King Khufu in about 2600 BC, were purely for ceremonial use. Built mainly of imported cedar wood, Khufu's barge was 141 ft (43 m) long and 20 ft (6 m) wide. When Khufu was buried at Giza in the Great Pyramid, his barge was dismantled and buried in a pit nearby to help him on his journey to the afterlife.

Early sails were made of papyrus, and later, linen.

Men with poles push the boat off sandbanks or away from the shore.

Single mast near the front of the boat

The boat's front is called the prow.

Khufu's royal cabin

Wooden framework for canopy

Khufu's boat had five pairs of oars, which give more power than paddles because they are much longer.

Model of Khufu's royal barge, c.2600 BC

Plumbline to test the depth of the water

c.2000 BC DOUBLE CANOE *Polynesia*

Four thousand years ago, Polynesian people set out from the islands of Southeast Asia to colonize other Pacific islands. They traveled great distances by raft or canoe. By placing two dugouts side by side and linking them with a deck, they made larger craft that were stable enough to carry sails without capsizing.

Sails made of palm leaves

Polynesian sailing craft, made of two linked dugouts

The body, or hull, was made of short wooden planks fixed side by side.

2000–1001 BC

•**3000 BC** In Mesopotamia, the yoke, a wooden board placed across the shoulders, is used so that oxen can pull heavy wagons.
•**3000 BC** People start to ride horses. They probably ride bareback, and control the horse with a rope tied around its lower jaw.
•**2500 BC** Swimmers in Egypt can do the crawl stroke as well as the breaststroke.

•**2500 BC** The Egyptians build boats made from short wooden planks.
•**2500 BC** Remains found in Khazakstan show that people are using snow skis.
•**2500 BC** A stone causeway, or raised road, 0.6 mile (1 km) long is built in Egypt over 10 years. Two million huge stones are dragged along it on sleds to build the Great Pyramid.
•**2500 BC** Warriors in Mesopotamia now have four-wheeled war chariots. The nomadic Hyksos people introduce faster, two-wheeled chariots to Egypt nearly 1,000 years later.
•**2300 BC** Canals are dug in Egypt so that ships can bypass the rapids at Aswan on the Nile River.

•**2000 BC** Roads are built on the island of Malta. They have grooves cut into them 4.3 ft (1.3 m) apart, forming a sort of "railroad" along which carts can be pulled.
•**2000 BC** Spoked wheels are used on vehicles in Mesopotamia. Spoked wheels reach Egypt by 1600 BC, and China by 1300 BC.
•**1900 BC** Work starts on the first long-distance "roads" in Europe. These tracks, linking northern Europe with the Mediterranean region, are a trade route for valuable materials such as tin and amber.

•**1400 BC** Wheeled vehicles are now in use in Europe, and spoked wheels are introduced there around 1000 BC.
•**1300 BC** Horse riders are now controlling their horses using a bit, a jointed metal band that fits inside the horse's mouth and is attached to the horse's headgear, or bridle.
•**1100 BC** Phoenician sailors learn to use the position of the stars to help them navigate their ships at night. They make star maps, and use the North Star to find north.

Early metal horse bit

1000 BC

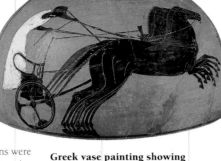

1000 BC	900 BC	800 BC	700 BC	600 BC		200 BC

LAND

Toy camel from Roman Egypt

c.550 BC
RACING CHARIOT *Greece*
Drawn by four galloping horses abreast, the Greek racing chariot was powerful, but hard to control and liable to skid on turns. In the Olympic Games, up to 40 chariots started a 9-mile (14-km) race, but spills and collisions were frequent, and few reached the finishing line. The prize went to the winning chariot's owner, not its driver.

Greek vase painting showing chariot racing, 6th century BC

Cover made of woven bamboo

Chinese oxcart

c.1000 BC CAMEL *Middle East*
In hot regions where there were no roads, and where food and water were scarce, the camel proved a more versatile means of transportation than the horse. Camels were first used for riding and as pack animals in the Middle East. Later, as more of the Sahara turned to sand, they were introduced into Africa, where long caravans of camels carried trading goods across the desert.

c.450 BC FOUR-HORSE CHARIOT *Persia*
Some chariots were fitted with larger wheels for a smoother ride over rough ground. Studs were sometimes attached around the rims of the wheels to make them less likely to slip. An exquisite gold model found near the Oxus River in central Asia shows a large-wheeled chariot pulled by four small horses attached to two poles.

Wheel strengthened to carry heavy loads

Triremes were crewed by up to 170 oarsmen in three tiers.

The oarsmen sat side-on, along the length of the ship.

Each oarsman rowed with a single oar.

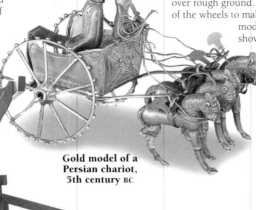

Gold model of a Persian chariot, 5th century BC

c.400 BC NOMADS' CART *Siberia*
The nomadic people who lived in the steppes, or grasslands, of central Asia used huge carts to carry their belongings as they moved from one place to another. When they stopped to set up camp, the top portion could be lifted down to form the framework of a tent.

Cart from Pazyryk, Siberia, 5th century BC

The two upper rows of oars were nearly 16 ft (5 m) long.

Cutaway model of a Greek trireme

c.500 BC
TRIREME *Greece*
By 800 BC, the Phoenicians were building biremes, fast, powerful galleys with two rows of oars on each side. They were followed by triremes, with three rows of oars on each side. By 500 BC, Greek triremes were up to 130 ft (40 m) long. A pointed ram fixed to the prow, or front, of the ship at the water-line was used to sink enemy ships by smashing a hole in their hulls. Triremes also carried archers and soldiers for boarding other vessels.

The wheels were 5 ft (1.6 m) across.

The lateen is called a fore-and-aft sail, because it runs along the boat from front to back.

The helmsman guided the boat using two long tillers attached to the steering oars.

WATER

c.1000 BC TRADING SHIP *Phoenicia*
By 1200 BC, warships and trading ships had begun to look very different. Warships, or galleys, were long, sleek, and low, powered by oarsmen as well as by sail. Trading ships were broader and deeper, and relied almost entirely on their sails. From 2000 to 350 BC, the Phoenicians were the most important traders in the Mediterranean. From their base at the eastern end of the Mediterranean (now Syria, Lebanon, and Israel), their wooden trading ships journeyed as far as northern Europe and Africa's west coast.

Sailors climbed the mast to look out for land.

The ship had a single, central mast with a square sail.

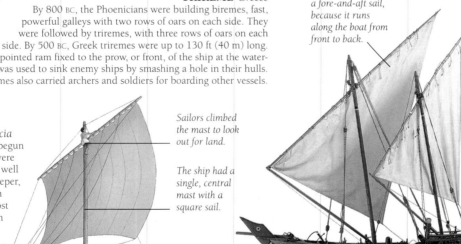

Cutaway of a Phoenician trading ship

c.200 BC
LATEEN-RIGGED CRAFT
Mediterranean region
The rectangular sails of early ships ran from side to side. Such sails were of little use if the wind was not blowing in the direction the ship had to go. Triangular lateen sails, running along the line of a ship from front to back, enabled ships to sail almost into the wind. Lateen sails first appeared in the Mediterranean region, and are still common on small ships called dhows.

Model dhow with lateen rigging

1000–501 BC		500–1 BC	

MILESTONES

•**1000 BC** The Chinese now have a network of roads with speed limits and officials to keep control. There are traffic regulations about how large vehicles can be, and who has priority at busy crossings.
•**1000 BC** Three thousand years before the first airplane, a Greek legend describes how Daedalus and Icarus try to escape from prison by making themselves wings from feathers fastened with thread and wax. Icarus flies too close to the Sun: the wax melts and he falls to his death. Daedalus lands safely in Sicily.

The cargo was lashed into place below deck.

The hull was made watertight by coating it with tar.

•**1000 BC** The Chinese begin to fly kites. Some are said to be so large that they can lift people into the air.
•**600 BC** In forested and wetland regions of England where the ground is soft, people lay down pieces of wood to build "trackways." This provides a firm surface for people and

The Pharos at Alexandria

•**500 BC** The Royal Road, a leveled track, runs for 1,600 miles (2,600 km) across the Persian Empire from Sardis (in what is now Turkey) to Susa (in Iran). Horseback messengers can travel the whole distance in nine days.
•**500 BC** A trade route later called the Silk Road is established, crossing Asia and linking China with Persia. Along it, merchants carry precious metals and stones, spices, glass, and pottery, as well as silk. Chinese inventions, such as paper and gunpowder, will eventually spread to Europe along this route, as will epidemics of infectious diseases.

•**400 BC** There are about 300 ports dotted around the coast of the Mediterranean Sea, used by fishermen and traders.
•**250 BC** The world's first large lighthouse, the Pharos, is completed at Alexandria in Egypt. The light of a fire burning at the top of this 400-ft (120-m) high tower guides sailors safely into port at night.
•**200 BC** Lateen-rigged sailing ships appear in the Mediterranean region.
•**55 BC** Roman soldiers build a 1,800-ft (550-m) long wooden bridge across the Rhine River in 10 days.

0

AD 500

c.0 OXCART *China*

Until 2,000 years ago, two-wheeled carts had a single pole, or shaft, at the front. Animals were attached in pairs, one either side of the pole, to pull the cart. The Chinese then began to build carts with two front shafts, enabling them to be pulled by a single animal. The animal stood between the shafts, and a wooden cross-piece called a yoke fitted over its shoulders.

Yoke fits over the ox's shoulders.

Ox stands between the two shafts.

Indian cart with oxen yoked to a central shaft

c.100 SADDLED HORSE *China*

Early horse riders would often throw a piece of cloth over a horse's back before mounting, but it was the Chinese who developed the first saddles, which made riding easier and safer. Made of stiff material such as leather, they were padded and shaped for comfort. Metal stirrups, which fit around the rider's feet, were also in use in China by this time.

Padded saddle   *Harness*

Chinese terra-cotta horse of the Tang era (AD 610–906)

Model of a Roman corbita, c.2nd century AD

Heraldic device

Cargo hold

A small foresail, hanging from a forward-leaning mast, made the ship easier to steer.

Anchor

c.0 CORBITA *Rome*

A fleet of sturdy, two-masted ships called corbitas sailed between the ports of the Roman Empire. To make more room for cargo, corbitas had pear-shaped hulls, broader toward the stern, or back, of the boat. The largest Roman ships carried more than 1100 tons (1,000 tonnes) of cargo, such as corn and wine, as well as large numbers of passengers. Some corbitas traveled as far as India.

Viking sled c.AD 850

A carved beechwood box, decorated with metal studs, was tied to the frame.

Curved oak runners

c.850 VIKING SLED *Scandinavia*

The Vikings found that journeys over rugged terrain were often easiest in winter, when snow covered uneven ground. Towed by horses, dogs, reindeer, or people on skis, a sled's runners glide easily over snow and ice, making it more efficient than a wheeled vehicle.

Arab horseman

c.700 ARABIAN HORSE

Arab influence spread far and wide as the Islamic Empire expanded in the 7th and 8th centuries. Camels were the main form of transportation, but horses were treasured for their speed and grace. They were used for fighting, sports, and hunting. Horses were carefully chosen for breeding in order to produce high-quality offspring. Arabian horses are small, tough, and intelligent, with a silky coat of hair.

Model of a Viking knarr, or trading ship

c.850 VIKING SHIPS *Norway*

The Vikings were intrepid sailors who even ventured across the Atlantic in their open ships. Viking fighting vessels, or long-ships, were narrow and swift, carrying up to sixty oarsmen on each side. Longships, or karvs, were also used for coastal travel. The karv found at Oseberg, Norway, was 70 ft (21 m) long and was buried in the grave of a wealthy woman – perhaps a queen. Viking trading boats, or knarrs, were broader and traveled mainly under sail with a much smaller crew. Their shallow hulls enabled them to travel far up rivers. Knarrs carried Viking settlers as far as Iceland and Greenland.

The decorated spiral "stem post" above the prow is carved into a snake's head.

The raised prow stops the ship from nose-diving into the water in rough weather.

Reconstruction of the Oseberg Viking ship, 9th century AD

Oar ports

Clinker hull of overlapping planks held together by iron rivets

The bottom of the hull is strengthened by a projecting backbone of timbers called a keel.

- •0–100 The Romans use horseshoes consisting of metal plates tied under a horse's hooves with strips of leather.
- •0–300 The padded saddle and the rigid stirrup are invented in China, along with the padded collar, which allows horses to pull heavier loads without choking themselves.
- •0–400 Fifty thousand miles (80,000 km) of straight roads are built to link the cities of the Roman Empire.
- •100 Chariot racing in Rome attracts crowds of up to 250,000 people. Bets are placed, and winning charioteers become popular heroes.
- •100 The rudder is in use on Chinese ships by now, but may have been invented earlier.

- •200 Metal ice skates are used in Scandinavia. Earlier skates may have been made of bone splinters strapped to leather boots.
- •250 The Maya civilization in Central America reaches its greatest development, but without the aid of pack animals or wheeled vehicles. Maya traders transport their goods on their backs or by canoe.
- •250 The Chinese invent the wheelbarrow. It reaches Europe 1,000 years later.

Viking boot and skate, 10th century AD

- •605 Work is completed on the first sections of China's Grand Canal. The canal will eventually be more than 600 miles (1,000 km) long, linking the Yangtse River with the north of the country. By the 8th century, ships on the canal will carry 2 million tons (tonnes) of goods each year.
- •875–985 The Vikings set out from Scandinavia in their longships to start settlements in Iceland and Greenland.

- •900 Iron horseshoes, which are nailed onto a horse's hooves, are widely used throughout Europe. They were probably developed at an earlier date by the Romans or the Celts.
- •984 Locks are used for the first time on China's Grand Canal. A lock is a compartment with a gate at each end that allows a barge to pass from a higher level of a canal to a lower level, and vice versa.

1000

1175

1000	1035	1070	1105	1175	1210	1245	1280	1315

LAND

c.1000 WARHORSE *Japan*
Japanese samurai warriors wore very light armor, so they were able to ride swift, light horses from the mountains of northern Japan. Samurai were expert horsemen, able to fire arrows accurately from a fast-moving horse. Later, European knights wore thicker, heavier metal armor into battle, which prevented the horses from moving fast. In fact, horses often wore armor as well, so they had to be large, and strong enough to carry up to 400 lb (180 kg).

The horse wears a colorful coat decorated with heraldic designs.

c.1200 WARHORSE *Europe*
Strength and steadiness were essential for both horse and knight in battle. These were acquired in a sport called jousting, which was also good battle training. Pairs of armored knights rode full-tilt toward one another, each with the aim of breaking his lance (a long, spearlike weapon) against his opponent's shield or knocking him off his horse.

Chain-mail armor

Reconstruction of a jousting knight, 14th century

Early samurai warrior

Farm cart with studded wheels, c.1340

c.1340 TWO-WHEELED CART *Europe*
Early harnesses tended to throttle horses if they pulled too hard when towing carts and wagons. By the 14th century, harnesses with padded collars were in common use in Europe, allowing horses to pull much harder without such danger. Cart wheels often had metal rims, called tires, as well as studs to prevent them from slipping sideways.

The sails are made of matting.

Most junks are three-masted, but larger ones have five.

The light armor was made of small, thin, iron plates, lacquered and laced together with silk and leather.

Four-sided lugsails hang from the masts at an angle.

WATER

The sails are stiffened with bamboo strips, keeping them flat and making it easy to fold up part of a sail in high winds.

Fighting cog, 1340

1340•
COG *Europe*
Cogs were tubby, single-masted ships that served both as cargo vessels and as warships. Their two castles, raised areas at the prow and the stern, made them easy to defend. Steered by a rudder and with a clinker-built hull (made from overlapping planks), sturdy cogs could withstand the rough North Atlantic seas.

Square bow

c.1000 JUNK *China*
Flat-bottomed boats called junks were developed in China more than 1,000 years ago. They were strongly built for sailing on the open seas of eastern Asia, and were used for both trading and fighting. At the stern they had a rudder, a flat plate under the boat that cuts through the water. The invention of the rudder was crucial to the development of larger ships, which could not be steered properly with oars.

The ship is steered by swiveling the sternpost rudder.

Model of a five-masted junk

The broad, flat hull has no keel.

1000–1174		1175–1349	

MILESTONES

•**1000** Wagons are built with a pivoted crossbar at the front called a whiffletree, to which harnesses are attached. It allows a team of horses to share the pulling of a wagon.
•**1002** Sailing west from Greenland, Norseman Leif Ericsson is believed to be the first European to visit North America.
•**1010** Oliver of Malmesbury, an English monk, jumps from a tower with wings on his hands and feet. He does not fly, but breaks his legs.

Chinese mariner's compass

•**1040** The recipe for "Black Powder," gunpowder rocket fuel, is published in China.
•**1100s** The Incas of South America start to build two roads, totaling 4,000 miles (6,400 km), to link parts of their empire. No wheeled vehicles will ever use these roads, just animals and people.
•**1119** Chinese sailors navigate with a "south-pointing needle," a compass made of a magnetized piece of iron floating in water. The iron turns to show magnetic north.

•**1187** Sailors in Europe are now using the magnetic compass.
•**1200** The sternpost rudder begins to appear on European ships, although it has been used before now on Chinese and Byzantine vessels.
•**1250** Roger Bacon, an English monk, writes a book in which he speculates about hollow globes that float in the air (balloons) and mechanical flying machines propelled by people riding on them.
•**1250** Single-masted sailing ships called cogs begin to appear in European waters.
•**1271** Seventeen-year-old Marco Polo from Venice sets out with his father and uncle on a journey across Asia that will last 24 years.

Wooden wing frame with netting support, perhaps for a covering of birds' feathers

•**1280** The Mediterranean lateen sail is now in use on European vessels.
•**1290** Marco Polo sees four-masted Chinese junks in China; ten years later he sees man-carrying kites in China.

1350

1525

1350 | 1385 | 1420 | 1455 | 1490 | 1525 | 1560 | 1595 | 1630

Replica of Elizabeth I's state coach, 1560

Man and pack horse wearing snowshoes, c.1550

c.1550 SNOWSHOES *Scandinavia*
People in cold countries learned to attach showshoes to their boots – and even to animal hooves – when walking on soft snow. Similar in shape and size to tennis rackets, snowshoes spread a person's weight and stop their feet from sinking into the snow.

1565•
LITTER *Peru*
A litter is a portable couch supported by long poles and carried by animals or by human bearers. Litters were important in Peru, because the Inca people had no wheeled vehicles. They were also widely used in Europe before comfortable wheeled coaches were available.

Litter carrying Inca emperor, 1565

1560•
STATE COACH *England*
In 1560, England's Queen Elizabeth I started a fashion when she acquired her own state coach. Soon, many other important women wanted their own luxury vehicles. Before this, royalty and wealthy people made journeys in bumpy "traveling carriages," which were little more than covered farm wagons.

Elephant armor, c.1600

c.1600 ARMORED ELEPHANT *India*
Because of their strength and size, elephants have been used in warfare since the time of Alexander the Great in the 4th century BC, and possibly before. They were sent into battle to terrify enemy troops and trample them. In India, they wore armor made of metal plates sewn onto a cloth backing.

Royal flag of Spain

The Santa Maria was probably a carrack, a small ship with three masts.

•1511 WARSHIP *Europe*
The age of great sea battles in Europe started with the development of gun-carrying warships, later called galleons. They had rows of guns on either side, placed low down to stop them from being top-heavy and liable to capsize. The guns were fired through holes cut into the ship's hull.

The English warship Mary Rose, built in 1511

c.1562 GONDOLA *Venice*
There were 10,000 gondolas in Venice in the 16th century carrying people around a city that has canals in place of streets. Today, there are a lot fewer of these sleek wooden boats, but they are still propelled by "gondoliers," who stand at the stern to operate a single long oar. According to a law passed in 1562, all gondolas must be painted black.

Stern oar

The metal fitting at the bow may have developed from a ram.

Venetian gondola

•1492 *SANTA MARIA* Spain
Christopher Columbus led his expedition across the Atlantic in an 80-ft (25-m) long ship called *Santa Maria*. Knowing that the Earth is round, Columbus aimed to reach the Far East by sailing westward from Europe. After more than a month at sea, land was sighted. However, it was not an Eastern land, but a "New World" unknown to people in Europe, later called America.

Model of the Santa Maria, 1492

•1620 SUBMARINE *England*
Several inventors tried to devise simple submarines. One of them was Cornelius Drebbel, a Dutchman working in London. It is claimed that his "diving boat" successfully traveled several miles up the Thames River in London. It was rowed by twelve oarsmen who were supplied with air through tubes from the surface.

Wooden submarine, 1683

1350–1524

"Ornithopter" based on the drawings of Leonardo da Vinci

•**1350–1450** Three-masted carrack ships slowly replace the smaller cogs. *See* COG **1340**.
•**1400** Wagons appear that have a body hung from the chassis, or main framework, by leather straps, giving a more comfortable ride.

•**1420** Henry the Navigator, a Portuguese prince, inspires sailors to explore the coast of Africa.
•**1492** Christopher Columbus makes the first of his four journeys to Central America and the Caribbean.
•**1497–8** From Portugal, Vasco da Gama sails around Africa to India.
•**1505** In Italy, Leonardo da Vinci starts a study of flight and makes drawings of flying machines.
•**1519** Hernando Cortés takes at least 16 horses from Spain to Mexico. Horses have been extinct on the American continent for 8,000 years.
•**1522** Ferdinand Magellan's *Vittoria* is the first ship to complete a round-the-world voyage.

1525–1699

•**1538** Primitive diving bells are used in Spain.
•**1550** High-sided ships called galleons are common in Europe. They are used as both fighting and trading ships.
•**1550** European noblemen are acquiring their own road vehicles, called coaches after the Hungarian town of Kocs.
•**1600** A program of road building starts in France. By 1664, the roads will be so good that a stagecoach service starts.
•**1600** About 600 carriages are available for hire in London, and 300 in Paris. In London, they are called hackneys.

•**1640** Sedans, enclosed chairs carried by two bearers, are popular in many European cities.
•**1650** A three-wheeled invalid carriage, with "pedals" turned by hand, is used by a disabled man, Stephen Farfler, in Nuremberg, Germany.
•**1662** A horse-drawn bus service starts in Paris, with set routes and schedules.
•**1675** Greenwich Observatory is set up near London. Its services will help seamen throughout the world navigate better.

1700   1720

| 1700 | 1704 | | | 1716 | 1720 | 1724 | |

LAND

c.1700 HORSEBACK WARRIOR *Nigeria*

In tropical Africa, the easiest way to travel was by river. For land travel, horses could not be used because they were attacked by the tsetse fly, which carried a fatal disease. This Benin warrior came from a part of Nigeria where the tsetse fly was rare, and the ruler kept an army that included many horsemen.

Bronze plaque of mounted Benin warrior, c.1700

c.1700 STAGE WAGON *England*

Lumbering stage wagons ran regularly on important cross-country routes, carrying a few passengers as well as several tons (tonnes) of goods. Ten or twelve horses were needed to pull these huge vehicles, which covered as much as 20 miles (32 km) a day in good weather. Stage wagons had broad wheels to stop them from sinking into mud, and were controlled by drovers who walked or rode alongside.

Stage wagon

c.1720 SEDAN CHAIR *Europe*

To beat traffic jams, wealthy people hired sedan chairs instead of coaches. Carried by two "chairmen," a sedan could go through streets too narrow for a coach. Sedans were also used on longer journeys. They were often elaborately decorated outside and luxurious within.

Sedan chair, c.1720

Wooden frame

Skin bag decorated with beads

North American Indian cradleboard, c.1850

Coal-carrying wagonway

c.1730 WAGONWAY *Europe*

The first "railroads" were wooden planks or metal plates laid down so that horses could pull wagons more easily. In the example above, a full wagon coasts downhill, controlled by a driver sitting on the brake lever. The horse will pull the wagon back up for the next load. A horse might also pull a full wagon uphill, then ride back down in an empty one.

•1735 TRANSPORTATION FOR CHILDREN

For his children, the Duke of Devonshire built a tiny carriage that could be pulled by a dog, goat, or pony. Baby carriages were later called perambulators or prams. But throughout history, most babies were carried on their mothers' backs in animal-skin pouches. A cradleboard, used by North American Indians, was a skin bag on a frame. It was strapped to the mother's back, hung from a saddle, or tied to a travois. *See* TRAVOIS c.1880.

Child's carriage made for Duke of Devonshire

WATER

Masts were made taller by adding extensions called topmasts.

Single square sail

The masts are supported at the sides by ladderlike arrangements of ropes called shrouds.

Mainmast

Mizzenmast

Foremast

The supporting ropes running fore and aft are called stays.

Model of a Japanese cargo vessel

c.1700 CARGO SHIP *Japan*

From 1639 to 1858, the Japanese government tried to preserve the country's culture and religion by banning all contact with the outside world. People were not allowed to leave the country, and the size of cargo ships was restricted so that they could not be sailed to foreign lands. The square-rigged vessel above had an opening in the stern into which the rudder was raised if the ship was at anchor. Similar ships were still being built early in the 20th century.

Bowsprit

•1733 WARSHIP *Europe*

In the 18th century, the galleon grew into a floating fortress. A large warship, called a "First-Rate" ship, had 100 guns, a crew of 850, and displaced 3,300 tons (3,000 tonnes) of water. Warships also carried more sails, supported by a forest of rigging. This made them faster and more maneuverable. In the Mediterranean Sea, galleys similar to those of ancient Greece could still be seen. Their many oarsmen enabled them to attack becalmed sailing boats, which could not escape when there was no wind. *See* WARSHIP 1511.

Fourth-Rate ship, 1733–1850

Maltese galley, c.1770

MILESTONES

1700–1739

•**1700** Ships known as East Indiamen bring valuable cargoes of ivory, spice, and silk from India, China, and the East Indies into European ports.

•**1710** Larger ships are now steered by turning a wheel on the deck. This is linked to a mechanism called a block and tackle, which moves the rudder.

•**1712** The first steam engine, of the type devised by Thomas Newcomen, starts working in England, where it is used to pump water from coal mines. After improvements by James Watt and others, coal-powered steam engines will revolutionize transportation.

A Fourth-Rate ship carried 50–70 guns (later 60–80) that mainly fired solid round shot made of iron.

•**1714** The British government offers a £20,000 prize for the first ship's clock that keeps accurate time at sea. The prize is won by John Harrison, with his No. 4 chronometer of 1759.

•**1716** The French establish the first national highways department.

•**1717** English astronomer Edmond Halley develops a diving bell with a system for refreshing the air in the bell.

John Harrison's 1759 No. 4 chronometer

The capstan – a large drum turned by spokelike poles – was used to wind in the anchor or raise the yards.

•**1730s** Wheels made from cast iron, a hard brittle metal, start to replace wooden ones on wagonways in Europe. Steam trains will later rely on all-metal wheels.

•**1731** In Philadelphia, a hand-operated pump is used to put out fires instead of a chain of water-filled buckets. Mounted on wheels, it is the first practical fire engine in the US.

•**1731** Englishman John Hadley invents the octant, which gives latitude at sea by measuring the height of the Sun or stars above the horizon.

•**1732** In England, the first lightship is anchored near the mouth of the Thames River. A lightship is an alternative to a lighthouse where it is not possible to build foundations. *See* LIGHTSHIP 1963.

•**1735** Swiss engineer Charles Dangeau de Labelye develops the caisson. This boxlike shell can be lowered onto a riverbed and pumped dry from inside, enabling engineers to build bridge foundations underwater.

1740

1760

1740	1744	1748	1752	1756	1760	1764	1768	1772

c.1740 POST CHAISE *France/England*

The lightweight "chaise de poste" carriage was first made in France in the 1660s. It was introduced to England in 1743, where it was called the post chaise. It was faster and more comfortable than a stagecoach, although the fare was far more expensive. With fresh horses hired from inns along the route, a post chaise could travel up to 50 miles (80 km) a day. It had no driver, but was controlled by men called post-boys or postilions, who rode the horses.

Post chaises at a coaching inn, c.1780

c.1760 ROLLER SKATE *Europe*

In 1760, a Belgian musician called Joseph Merlin caused a sensation in London when he entered a fancy-dress ball on roller skates while playing the violin. Unable to stop, he crashed into a £500 mirror and broke it. Merlin's roller skates, made for his own amusement, were not the first. Roller skates were probably invented in Holland at the start of the 18th century. These "ground skates," as they were known, consisted of a rigid, wheeled sole that was attached to a shoe. They were almost impossible to steer around corners.

Dutch engraving of a roller skater, 1790

Steam was produced by heating water in a huge copper boiler.

Steam pipe

High-pressure steam from the boiler drove pistons in two bronze cylinders.

The driver turned the tiller to steer the vehicle.

The two rear wheels and the front driving wheel had broad, iron tires around their rims.

Chimney

Brake pedal

Model of Cugnot's steam-powered *Fardier*, 1769

Seat

Log basket

Carrying fork to hold the boiler, which was so heavy it made the vehicle unstable

The pistons powered a single front driving wheel, via a ratchet mechanism.

•1769 STEAM-POWERED TRACTOR *France*

In the late 18th century, several people tried to make steam-powered road vehicles. The first to succeed was Nicholas Cugnot, a French army engineer. His three-wheeled tractor was the first self-propelled vehicle – that is, able to move under its own power. Designed as a gun carriage, it reached a speed of 3 mph (5 kph) in 1770, pulling a 3-ton cannon. But Cugnot's hefty tractor, or *Fardier*, was unstable. It capsized in a Paris street, demolishing a wall, and was not used again.

c.1770 BARK CANOE *Australia*

Since the earliest days of water travel, people have made boats out of long, wide strips of bark peeled from trees such as birch or eucalyptus. With its ends tied up, the bark naturally takes the shape of a simple but effective canoe. Bark canoes are fast, strong, and light enough to be carried overland on parts of a journey where they cannot be paddled.

Aboriginal eucalyptus canoe, Australia, painted, c.1770

c.1750 CARGO SHIP *Europe*

By the mid-18th century, cargo ships were transporting people, animals, and goods all over the world. When horses had to be taken abroad, they were loaded like other cargo into the ship's hold, where they stood on sand to protect their hooves. Cargo was hoisted onto the ship using one of the yards as a crane. The cargo was carefully loaded both to make sure it did not move in stormy seas, and to balance the ship.

The yard was used as a crane.

Horse lowered into the hold on a harness

Model of an 18th-century cargo ship

Horse-drawn canal barge

c.1760 CANAL BARGE *Europe*

As countries in Europe became more industrial, canal traffic increased between important trade centers, and new canals were dug. Loads can be moved more easily on water than on land, so barges towed by horses became an efficient (if slow) way of transporting heavy cargos such as coal, farm produce, or pottery.

1776• SUBMARINE *US*

The first underwater ship used in war was the *Turtle*, designed by an American named David C. Bushnell. The *Turtle* carried one person, who maneuvered the craft with two propellers turned by hand. Like all submarines, it was made to sink or rise in the water by pumping water into and out of tanks inside the craft. The *Turtle*'s attempts to attach explosive mines to the British warship HMS *Eagle* off New York were unsuccessful.

Cutaway model of the *Turtle*, 1776

1740–1759		1760–1779	

•**1747** The School of Bridges and Highways is set up in France to train engineers in road-building techniques.
•**1748** Jacques Vaucanson, a French engineer, demonstrates a clockwork-powered carriage to the King of France.
1750s Many roads in England are now "turnpikes." Tolls are charged on these roads, and the money is used to improve them. The first turnpike in the US will be a new road built in Virginia in 1785.
•**1750** In England, James Heath devises the "bath-chair" as transportation for sick or disabled people. It is a small three-wheeled vehicle that is pushed from behind.

•**1756** Stagecoach services are in operation in North America by now.
•**1757** John Campbell, an English sailor, invents the sextant, a version of the octant that is more versatile and easy to use. *See* **MILESTONES 1731**.
•**1759** John Smeaton builds a new lighthouse on the dangerous Eddystone Rocks in the English Channel. It is the first to be built with underwater-setting cement and dovetailed stones, cut to fit into each other like pieces of a jigsaw puzzle.

Sextant

•**1761** Completion of the first part of the Bridgewater Canal in England starts a craze for canal building. This stretch includes the first boat-carrying aqueduct.
•**1768** In his ship *Endeavour*, the English Captain James Cook sets off on the first of three voyages during which he will explore Australia, New Zealand, Antarctica, and many Pacific islands.
•**1769** In France, Cugnot's ponderous steam tractor becomes the first self-propelled road vehicle.

•**1769** James Watt, a Scot, patents a steam engine that is six times more efficient than Thomas Newcomen's (*see* **MILESTONES 1712**). Watt will patent his improved "rotative" steam engine in 1782.
•**1776** David C. Bushnell's one-person submarine, *Turtle*, takes part in the American Revolutionary War.
•**1779** Abraham Darby III builds the world's first iron bridge over the Severn River at Coalbrookdale in England.
•**1778** Captain Cook arrives in Hawaii and sees surfboards in use there. Hawaiians call surfing "wave-sliding."

1780–1879 Full steam ahead

How much speed can the human body stand? People asked this question when the first steam trains were built, because they were worried that trains might go so fast that any passengers would be unable to breathe or would be shaken unconscious by the vibrations. But by the 1850s, train passengers were traveling at previously unheard-of speeds – 50 mph (80 kph) or more – and loving it!

Trains were also more comfortable than other forms of transportation, and less likely to grind to a halt in bad weather. Rail travel was cheap, so that people who had never been on a trip before could now afford to go by train. Places that had once seemed far apart suddenly felt much closer because people and goods could move between them in hours rather than days. In some places, new towns sprang up alongside the tracks. Even time itself was affected. Before railroads came, every town kept its own time, different from the time in towns just a few miles away. But when linked by rail, all clocks in a given area began to run on standard "railroad time."

Model of Richard Trevithick's "Catch Me Who Can" locomotive, 1808

The steam age

The invention of the steam engine provided transportation with a new energy source. Fueled by burning coal or wood, the first steam engines were huge, lumbering machines that rocked back and forth like see-saws. By the early 1800s, Richard Trevithick in England and Oliver Evans in the US had developed high-pressure engines that were small enough to mount on wheels, yet powerful

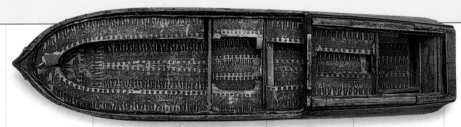

German horse-drawn wagonway, late 18th century

THE RAILROAD AGE

Before the invention of the steam engine, heavy loads were carried in wagons running on wooden planks, pulled either by horses or people. But steam locomotives proved far more powerful, and with smoother, stronger rails, they were also much faster. After the first steam locomotives of the early 1800s, railroads expanded rapidly, with a dramatic impact on daily life in many countries.

Steam whistle

Driver's cab

Coal-carrying tender

THE CHANGING WORLD: 1780–1879

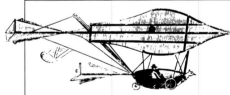

Sketch of Cayley's glider, 1853

SCIENCE AND TRANSPORTATION

By 1840, the word "scientist" had been devised to describe people who carry out experiments to discover how nature works. Scientific discoveries soon played an important role in the development of transportation. The work of Michael Faraday in England and Joseph Henry in the US, for example, showed how electricity could be used to power motors, which would one day drive streetcars and trains. And as early as 1809, English experimenter Sir George Cayley outlined the basic rules that enable machines to fly.

EXPANDING CITIES

During the 19th century, cities expanded rapidly as people moved from farm work to factory jobs. The populations of a number of cities grew to more than 1 million. Many people could no longer live near enough to the center to be able to walk to work, so new transportation systems were developed. Horse-drawn buses and streetcars were soon joined by electric streetcars and railroads running underground or overhead.

New York elevated railroad, late 19th century

Model of the slave ship *Brookes*, used by anti-slavery campaigners, c.1790

NEW INVENTIONS

The 19th century was a time of great technological change. Some inventors published their plans for machines that might speed up travel or save labor in the factory or the home. Others went straight ahead and turned their ideas into reality, building steam vehicles or outlandish bicycles, for example, and trying them out in public. Many inventions were instant failures – but not all. The elevator, or lift, and its later rival the escalator, soon caught on, and are still "people-movers" today.

Otis elevator

RELUCTANT TRAVELERS

Not everyone who traveled did so willingly. From England, convicted criminals were exiled to Australia, where they faced harsh conditions. And, over the course of 300 years, European "traders" forcibly shipped 10 million innocent Africans to the West Indies and countries in North and South America, where they were sold as slaves. Slave ships carried several hundred people chained below deck in appalling conditions. Many died during the long journey.

enough to drive the wheels themselves. These "locomotives" were set to work on railroads, and they soon put horse-drawn stagecoaches out of business. Some inventors developed steam road carriages, but they were heavy vehicles, difficult to maneuver on uneven roads. After several accidents, they became unpopular. On water, steam engines were used first to turn the paddle wheels and then the propellers of ships. But steam was slow to overtake wind power. Magnificent sailing ships continued to make their stately way across the world's oceans throughout the 19th century.

A new dimension

Ballooning caused as much sensation as the early railroads. "Aeronauts" rose above admiring crowds in the 1780s, lifted first by hot air, then by hydrogen gas. Ballooning was not yet a serious form of transportation – balloonists were at the mercy of the wind and had little control over where they landed. A number of inventors experimented with gliders and other types of aircraft. But proper powered flight could not be achieved with steam engines. By 1880, a more compact engine, the internal combustion engine, had been developed. It would have a huge effect on transportation in the next century.

Model of an American coal-burning locomotive of 1875

Steam dome

Warning bell

The "cowcatcher" pushes aside roaming animals such as cattle and buffalo.

TRANSPORTATION TECHNOLOGY

FLOATING ON AIR

Like fish in water, balloons float in air because their weight exactly balances the weight of the material they displace. Air expands when it is heated, so a balloonful of hot air is lighter than the same volume of cold air. If the combined weight of the balloon, its passengers and ballast, and the hot air inside it equals the weight of cold air that would fill the same space, the balloon will float. Heat the air a little more, or throw out some ballast, and the balloon will rise. Allow the air inside the balloon to cool, and it will gradually sink to the ground.

The Montgolfier brothers' hot-air balloon *Flesselles*, 1784

HIGH-PRESSURE STEAM

Energy had been locked away in coal for millions of years before the steam engine came along to convert it into something more useful – the ability to drive machines. When coal or other fuel is burned in the boiler of a steam engine, the heat released changes water into steam. Because the steam in the boiler is under high pressure, it carries a lot of energy. When the steam flows into a cylinder, its pressure pushes back a piston – rather like a bicycle pump works. The back-and-forth movement of the piston can be harnessed, via a crank, to turn the wheels that drive a ship's propeller, move a locomotive, or run machines in a factory.

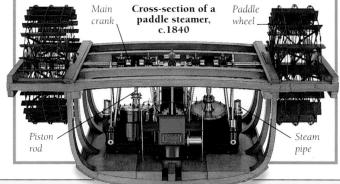

Main crank

Cross-section of a paddle steamer, c.1840

Paddle wheel

Piston rod

Steam pipe

ENGINEERING FEATS

The work of civil engineers was vital to the spread of railroads, roads, and canals. Using new construction techniques and materials, engineers were able to plan routes across even the most difficult terrain. They built stronger bridges, longer tunnels, and more durable roads. Successful engineers became popular heroes. But they also had to be good at persuading people to finance their daring schemes. Engineering failures, such as the collapse of a bridge, were not uncommon – and neither were financial failures.

A train emerges from a railroad tunnel in England, late 19th century

American settlers in a "prairie schooner" wagon, 1859

MASS MIGRATION

At a time when most people had never traveled more than a few miles from home, 10 million Europeans crossed the Atlantic to settle in North America. Another 10 million moved south to Australia, South America, and other countries. They traveled cheaply but uncomfortably by ship, driven out by overcrowding and poverty in Europe, and lured by the chance to make a new start. Pioneer settlers in the US still faced long overland journeys before they reached their destinations.

Child's tricycle, 19th century

IRON AND STEEL

A new way of making iron – using coke in the furnace instead of charcoal – was crucial to the industrialization of Europe and North America. Iron was used to make the cylinders of early steam engines, and the first metal rails on wagonways. Later, steel, a tough metal made by adding carbon and other materials to iron, became available. Steel is used to make ships, tools, railroad tracks, and girders.

The Iron Bridge at Coalbrookdale, England, c.1790

PLEASURE TRAVEL

Transportation developments in the 19th century gave many people the opportunity to travel for fun. Railroad companies organized outings to the seaside, called excursions, and weekend river trips by paddle-boat were enjoyed by millions. For the wealthier, the new railroads made foreign travel a pleasure rather than an ordeal. But in the days before the automobile, it was cycling that became the really affordable leisure activity. It was an ideal way to see the countryside and keep fit at the same time.

1780

1790

AIR

•1783
HOT-AIR BALLOON *France*
The French brothers Étienne and Joseph Montgolfier began a new era in transportation on November 21, 1783, when their vast hot-air balloon became the first to fly freely with people on board. With its two passengers, Pilâtre de Rozier and the Marquis d'Arlandes, the balloon made a safe landing after a 25-minute flight that took them 5.5 miles (9 km) across Paris.

Model of the Montgolfier brothers' balloon, 1783

Bath mail coach, 1784

1784•
MAIL COACH *England*
Mail services were greatly improved when letters began to be carried in special coaches, rather than on horseback. Mail coaches were faster than stagecoaches and, with an armed guard alongside the driver, they were less likely to be robbed.

LAND

Model of Murdock's tricycle

•1784 STEAM TRICYCLE *England*
A steam-powered three-wheeler, less than 1.6 ft (0.5 m) high, was built by William Murdock, one of James Watt's assistants. It hissed its way successfully through the streets of Redruth, in Cornwall, England. Murdock planned a full-size version, powerful enough to pull a carriage, but it was never built.

The small burner boiled water to produce steam.

•1786
STEAMBOAT *US*
American inventor John Fitch pioneered the use of steam power to drive riverboats. One of his early experimental boats had 12 vertical oars that were moved back and forth by the steam engine. A later version provided passenger service between Pennsylvania and New Jersey on the Delaware River, but it went out of business after a few months. Fitch also experimented with propeller-driven craft.

WATER

Fitch's steamboat on the Delaware River, 1786

Garnerin's parachute descent, 1797

•1797
PARACHUTE DESCENT *France*
On October 22, 1797, the Frenchman André-Jacques Garnerin made the first parachute descent from an aircraft. He bravely cut himself loose from a hydrogen balloon at a height of 2,300 ft (700 m) over Paris. His canvas parachute, 40 ft (12 m) across, opened perfectly, but swung violently from side to side as it came down. Garnerin was air-sick, but otherwise unharmed. Later parachutes had a hole in the center to let the air inside escape and stop them from swinging.

c.1790
STAGECOACH
Europe
Gaudily painted stagecoaches ran regular services between towns and cities. Passengers often got an uncomfortable ride as they traveled over bumpy roads. More people rode on the outside of a coach than inside, making it liable to overturn. "Outsiders" had fresh air and fine views, but were more likely to be hurt in accidents and occasionally froze to death in wintry weather.

Boarding a stagecoach

The outrigger is connected to the hull by a platform. This canoe even has a hut built on the platform.

Under sail, the wooden outrigger skims the water's surface.

Model of "Tepuke" canoe, Solomon Islands

c.1790 OUTRIGGER *Pacific Islands*
Pacific island peoples made ocean journeys in dugouts fitted with sails. Dugouts are unstable under sail, so a float called an outrigger was often added to the hull. An outrigger is kept facing the wind (windward) to balance the pressure of the wind on the sail. If it were away from the wind (leeward), the wind would force it underwater, tearing it from the hull.

The crew members transfer their weight to the leeward side to stop the float from being submerged.

Outrigger canoes have a symmetrical hull, with no fixed bow or stern. To change direction, the sail is reset at the other end of the canoe.

MILESTONES

•**1780s** Copper plates are fitted to the bottoms of ships' hulls to protect them from worms, barnacles, and weeds that slow them down.
•**1783** On November 21, the Montgolfier brothers' hot-air balloon carries the first two people ever to fly. On December 1, two more Frenchmen, Professor Charles and his mechanic Robert, make the first flight in a hydrogen balloon. Balloon ascents will follow in Italy and England in 1784; Holland, Belgium, and Germany in 1785; and the US in 1793.
•**1783** In France, Sebastien Lenormand makes parachute descents from a tree and a tower.
•**1783** The Marquis Jouffroy d'Abbans builds a successful steam paddleboat in France.

•**1784** In England, a regular mail coach service (probably the world's first) starts from London to Bath. Mail coaches are exempt from road tolls.

Fan commemorating Charles's first balloon flight, 1783

•**1790s** Trade between Europe and the Far East is now carried by ships of 1,300 tons (1,200 tonnes) or more called East Indiamen. One East Indiaman, the *Essex*, can set as many as 63 separate sails.
•**1792** In France, the emperor Napoleon's surgeon devises a horse-drawn ambulance to carry wounded soldiers. It has springs to smooth the ride over bumpy ground.
•**1794** A ball bearing is patented by Philip Vaughan in England. Ball bearings enable wheels to turn more easily and will become important in the development of the bicycle and other machines.

•**1796** Wooden warships *Constitution* and *President* are launched in the US, and are the largest and best of their type.
•**1797** Richard Trevithick in England and Oliver Evans in the US start to develop high-pressure steam engines, which will eventually make steam railroads possible.
•**1797** In Paris, André-Jacques Garnerin makes the first free parachute descent from a balloon.
•**1799** The first design for an airplane is sketched by English nobleman Sir George Cayley. It has a fixed wing, a separate tail, a rudder for side-to-side control, and elevators for up-and-down control.

1800

1810

1800   1804   1806   1808   1810   1812

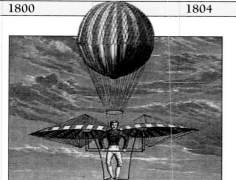

Degen's ornithopter, 1809

1809•
ORNITHOPTER *Austria*
Over the centuries, many people have tried to copy the way birds fly, but all without success. Some attached feathers to their bodies and attempted to glide from the tops of towers. Most were injured as they fell to the ground. Others ran along, flapping their "wings" as they tried to get airborne. Mechanical flapping-machines called ornithopters were also used. Jacob Degen, a Swiss inventor living in Vienna, managed to get his ornithopter off the ground – but only because it was attached to a hydrogen balloon.

So much smoke and noise came from the chimney that people complained.

Madame Blanchard falls to her death

•1819
BALLOON ACCIDENT
France
Before a huge crowd in Paris, Marie-Madeleine Blanchard, the first professional woman balloonist, gave a fireworks display from a hydrogen balloon in 1819. All was going well as she ascended in a "golden rain" of sparks and fire. But hydrogen from the balloon suddenly caught fire, and Madame Blanchard was killed as the balloon plunged to the ground.

The sail, made of matting, is a specialized type of lateen.

Piston rod

Steam produced in the boiler moved the pistons, which, in turn, powered the driving wheels.

Furnace

Coal wagon

•1805
STEAM VEHICLE *US*
Oliver Evans, an American engineer, mounted a high-pressure steam engine in a flat-bottomed boat for use as a dredger in the Schuylkill River. To reach the river, he fitted the boat with wheels and used the steam engine to drive it 1.2 miles (2 km) along the streets of Philadelphia. This strange amphibious craft was the first self-propelled vehicle in the United States.

The distinctive shape of the "crab-claw" or "half-moon" sail helps keep the sail flat in strong winds.

Hedley's locomotives and wagons had flanged wheels.

Puffing Billy, 1813

•1817 RUNNING
MACHINE *Germany*
One of the earliest ancestors of the bicycle was the "running machine," devised by a German Baron named Karl von Drais. It had no brakes or pedals. Riders sat on the saddle, leaned forward on a padded support, and propelled themselves forward with huge strides of their legs. In Britain it was called the "hobby horse." Riders could reach speeds of up to 9.5 mph (15 kph).

Hobby horse, c.1820

•1813
PUFFING BILLY *England*
Some railroad builders thought the new steam locomotives would not grip the iron track well enough to haul long, heavy trains. But William Hedley, the engineer of a horse-drawn railroad in the north of England, proved them wrong. He converted his railroad to steam, building locomotives that could haul 50-ton trains of coal wagons.

Oliver Evans's steam vehicle 1805

The ship is called a lugger because it is rigged with angled lugsails.

The paddle wheels were detached and laid on the deck when the ship was under sail.

•1800 LUGGER *Europe*
Many varieties of small vessels have been used for sailing close to the shore, for example by fishermen or to carry loads from port to port around the coast. The special feature of the type known as a "lugger" was its trapezoidal sails set almost fore-and-aft along the line of the boat. Luggers were particularly popular with smugglers, who needed to bring their contraband ashore at places where there was no proper harbor.

Model of a French lugger, c.1800

Model of *Savannah*, 1819

1819•
SAVANNAH *US*
The *Savannah* combined sail and steam power. Its masts could be fully rigged, but it also had paddle wheels, powered by a small steam engine, to keep it moving when the wind was not right for sailing. In 1819, *Savannah* became the first "steamer" to cross the Atlantic, but it relied on sails alone for most of the journey.

1800–1809

1810–1819

Military rockets, 1806

•**1800s** The "Coaching Age" approaches its height in Europe. Many new types of private coach are introduced, and the roads, which are being improved, are very busy with horse-drawn traffic.
•**1801** Richard Trevithick runs a steam road carriage at 8 mph (13 kph) in Cornwall, England. It eventually catches fire after he lets the engine boil dry.
•**1803** The world's first public railroad opens near London, England. Its horse-drawn trains carry goods only. The first railroad for fare-paying passengers, also horse-drawn, opens at Oystermouth in South Wales a few years later.

•**1803** In England, Richard Trevithick builds the first steam railroad locomotive.
•**1804** Coach travel improves with the invention of elliptical metal suspension springs by Obadiah Elliot in England. They will later be used on automobiles.
•**1806** Rockets are used for the first time in European warfare. The British fire 2,000 of them against the French in 30 minutes.
•**1807** The first reliable steamboat, Robert Fulton's *Clermont*, operates on the Hudson River in the US.

•**1812** Commercial steamboats begin to run on the Mississippi River in the US.
•**1813** William Hedley shows that locomotives with metal wheels can pull trains on metal rails without slipping. The wheels have a lip, or flange, that fits inside the flat rail to guide the train.
•**1816–20** John McAdam, a Scot, develops an improved method of surfacing roads. He and his sons will build 2,000 miles (3,200 km) of roads in the UK. His method will be widely used elsewhere.

•**1817** In Germany, Baron von Drais devises his "Draisine" running machine.
•**1818** The US government builds a road called the "National Pike" linking towns in Maryland and West Virginia – possibly the first major US highway.
•**1818** French-born Marc Isambard Brunel invents a tunnel-boring machine.
•**1819** The Danish scientist Hans Christian Oersted discovers the link between magnetism and electricity. In 1821, Englishman Michael Faraday will use this discovery to make the first electric motor, although it will have no real practical use. *See* **MILESTONES 1831**.

1820   1825

| 1820 | 1821 | 1822 | 1823 | 1824 | 1825 | 1826 | 1827 | 1828 | 1829 |

AIR

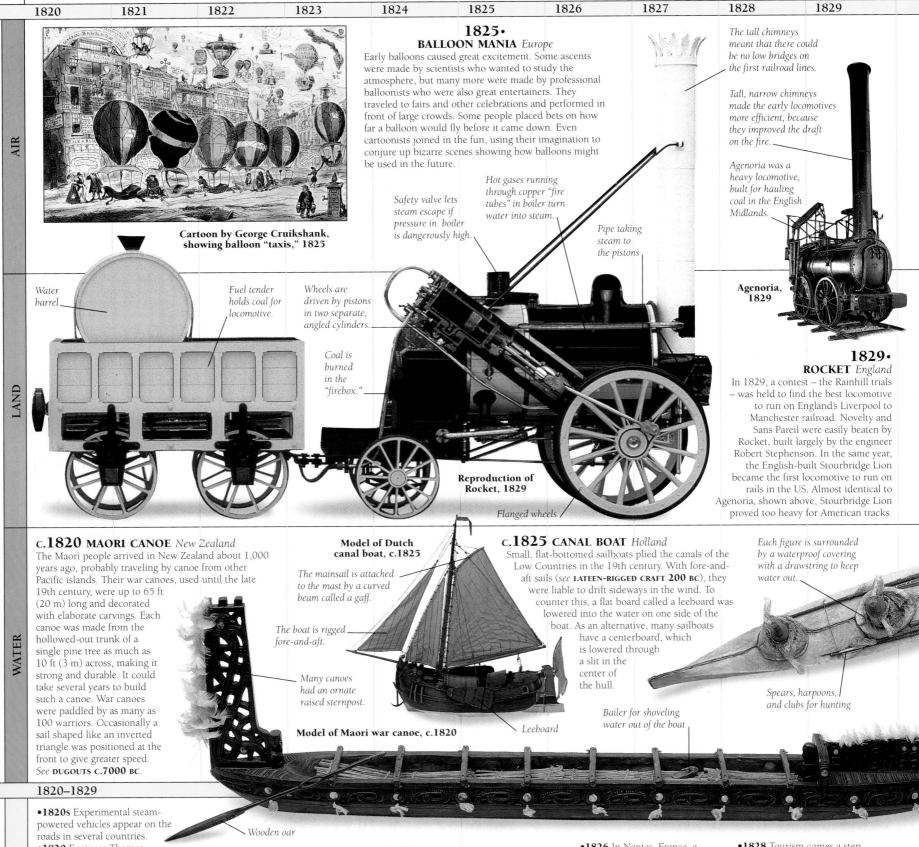

Cartoon by George Cruikshank, showing balloon "taxis," 1825

1825•
BALLOON MANIA *Europe*
Early balloons caused great excitement. Some ascents were made by scientists who wanted to study the atmosphere, but many more were made by professional balloonists who were also great entertainers. They traveled to fairs and other celebrations and performed in front of large crowds. Some people placed bets on how far a balloon would fly before it came down. Even cartoonists joined in the fun, using their imagination to conjure up bizarre scenes showing how balloons might be used in the future.

The tall chimneys meant that there could be no low bridges on the first railroad lines.

Tall, narrow chimneys made the early locomotives more efficient, because they improved the draft on the fire.

Agenoria was a heavy locomotive, built for hauling coal in the English Midlands.

Agenoria, 1829

LAND

Water barrel

Fuel tender holds coal for locomotive.

Wheels are driven by pistons in two separate, angled cylinders.

Safety valve lets steam escape if pressure in boiler is dangerously high.

Hot gases running through copper "fire tubes" in boiler turn water into steam.

Pipe taking steam to the pistons

Coal is burned in the "firebox."

Reproduction of Rocket, 1829

Flanged wheels

1829•
ROCKET *England*
In 1829, a contest – the Rainhill trials – was held to find the best locomotive to run on England's Liverpool to Manchester railroad. Novelty and Sans Pareil were easily beaten by Rocket, built largely by the engineer Robert Stephenson. In the same year, the English-built Stourbridge Lion became the first locomotive to run on rails in the US. Almost identical to Agenoria, shown above, Stourbridge Lion proved too heavy for American tracks.

WATER

c.1820 MAORI CANOE *New Zealand*
The Maori people arrived in New Zealand about 1,000 years ago, probably traveling by canoe from other Pacific islands. Their war canoes, used until the late 19th century, were up to 65 ft (20 m) long and decorated with elaborate carvings. Each canoe was made from the hollowed-out trunk of a single pine tree as much as 10 ft (3 m) across, making it strong and durable. It could take several years to build such a canoe. War canoes were paddled by as many as 100 warriors. Occasionally a sail shaped like an inverted triangle was positioned at the front to give greater speed.
See **DUGOUTS C.7000 BC.**

Model of Dutch canal boat, c.1825

The mainsail is attached to the mast by a curved beam called a gaff.

The boat is rigged fore-and-aft.

Many canoes had an ornate raised sternpost.

Model of Maori war canoe, c.1820

c.1825 CANAL BOAT *Holland*
Small, flat-bottomed sailboats plied the canals of the Low Countries in the 19th century. With fore-and-aft sails (*see* **LATEEN-RIGGED CRAFT 200 BC**), they were liable to drift sideways in the wind. To counter this, a flat board called a leeboard was lowered into the water on one side of the boat. As an alternative, many sailboats have a centerboard, which is lowered through a slit in the center of the hull.

Bailer for shoveling water out of the boat

Leeboard

Each figure is surrounded by a waterproof covering with a drawstring to keep water out.

Spears, harpoons, and clubs for hunting

Wooden oar

MILESTONES

1820–1829

•**1820s** Experimental steam-powered vehicles appear on the roads in several countries.
•**1820** Engineer Thomas Telford has now constructed 930 miles (1,500 km) of new roads in the UK. This includes the building of 1,117 bridges.
•**1821** In England, Charles Green makes the first ascent in a balloon filled with coal gas.
•**1822** French engineer Marc Seguin builds an experimental "suspension" bridge that hangs from wire cables.

•**1825** The Stockton to Darlington railroad opens in England. Trains run on 10-ft (3-m) iron rails and cross the first iron railroad bridge.
•**1825** In France, Marc Seguin invents the fire-tube boiler to make steam locomotives more efficient.
•**1825** The 360-mile (580-km) Erie Canal opens in the US. It enables boats to travel from the Atlantic Ocean to the Great Lakes.

The Erie Canal

•**1826** In Nantes, France, a Monsieur Baudry runs a regular passenger service in a horse-drawn vehicle that he calls an "omnibus."
•**1827** In France, Onésiphore Pecqueur invents "differential" gearing, allowing wheels on one side of a vehicle to turn faster than those on the other side when turning corners. It will later be used for automobiles.

•**1828** Tourism comes a step nearer when Karl Baedeker publishes a guidebook in Germany. It is called *The Rhine from Mainz to Cologne.*
•**1829** A competition at Rainhill in England to find the best steam locomotive is won by Robert Stephenson's Rocket.
•**1829** Stourbridge Lion, a British-built locomotive, is the first to run in the US, but is not a success.

1830

1830	1831	1832	1833	1834

1835

1835	1836	1837	1838	1839

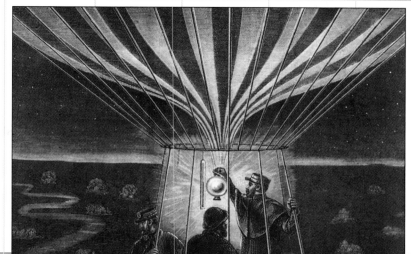

Best Friend of Charleston

•1830 BEST FRIEND OF CHARLESTON US
The first American-built locomotives were usually lighter than English ones, and some had the boiler, in which water is changed to steam, mounted vertically instead of horizontally. Best Friend of Charleston pulled trains on the South Carolina Railroad until a mechanic one day held down the safety valve, causing the boiler to explode violently. It was later rebuilt and its name changed to Phoenix.

Model kayak

c.1830 KAYAK Alaska
When European traders and explorers visited the Arctic, they saw Inuit people hunting sea otters from skin-covered canoes called kayaks. These boats had probably changed very little in hundreds of years. To keep out water, the kayak's wooden frame was completely covered with seal skin, leaving only small openings for people to sit in. The three-person kayak may have been developed by Russian traders from smaller Inuit kayaks. Skin-covered kayaks are still used today in Greenland.

Carved figurehead at front of canoe

Sansons' dirigible, 1839

Royal Vauxhall's long-distance flight, 1836

1836•
LONG-DISTANCE BALLOON England
The English aeronaut Charles Green's greatest balloon was the *Royal Vauxhall*. Made from 6,070 ft (1,850 m) of Italian silk and standing 80 ft (25 m) high, it was filled with coal gas. On November 7, 1836, Green and two companions took off from London in the *Royal Vauxhall*. Their record-breaking flight ended the next morning 480 miles (770 km) away, near Weilburg in the Duchy of Nassau (now part of Germany).

•1835
PHAETON Europe/US
By the early 19th century, there was a vast array of different private carriages from which to choose, with styles to suit every occasion. With its high seat and open top, the elegant four-wheeled phaeton was the carriage for people who wanted to look fashionable around town. First used in France, the phaeton also became popular in England and the US.

Phaeton, c.1835

1839•
DIRIGIBLE BALLOON
France
Ballooning could not be a serious form of transportation until it was possible to build "airships" or "dirigibles" – balloons that could be steered as they flew. The first step was to change the balloon's shape, making a long balloon that cut more easily through the air. The second step was to find a means of propulsion. Suggestions included propellers turned by the passengers and jets of hot air blowing out at the back. The Sansons, a French father and son team, planned a dirigible driven by flapping wings and paddle wheels.

•1838
MULE CART
India
Small carts have changed very little in 3,000 years. The mule cart below is from rural India, where it was used for personal transportation and for carrying farm produce to market. A mule is the offspring of a female horse and a male donkey. Hardy and sure-footed, mules can withstand both heat and cold, and can walk up to 50 miles (80 km) in a day.

Indian mule cart, 1838

•1838 SIRIUS Ireland
Sirius was the first ship to cross the Atlantic entirely under its own steam. But it nearly ran out of coal, and only completed the journey by burning its cabin furniture, spare yards, and one mast in order to keep the steam up in its boiler. *Sirius* left Cork, Ireland, on April 4, reaching New York after 18 days and 10 hours at sea. The *Great Western*, a more powerful steamship, arrived 4 hours later, having crossed from Bristol, England, in just 15 days. The *Great Western* was specially designed for transatlantic voyages, so it still had plenty of coal left when it reached New York. *See* SAVANNAH 1819.

Model of *Sirius*, 1838

1836•
EAST INDIAMAN Europe
For more than 200 years, trade between Europe and Asia was dominated by "East India companies" based in Europe. Their magnificent sailing ships were called East Indiamen. These armed trading ships carried gold and silver on the outward journey, and brought back jewelry, spices, tea, porcelain, and furniture to Europe.

East Indiaman, 1836

1830–1834	1835–1839

•**1830** The Liverpool to Manchester line in England is the first to provide a regularly scheduled service with steam-powered passenger and freight trains. The trains soon replace the local stagecoach service because they are cheaper and quicker.
•**1830** Best Friend of Charleston is the first successful steam locomotive to be built in the US. In 1831, it reaches 25 mph (40 kph) on its first run in South Carolina.
•**1830** The first railroad tunnel is built on England's Canterbury to Whitstable line.
•**1830** America's first successful balloonist, Charles Durant, makes his maiden flight from New York.

•**1831** The engineer Marc Seguin's steam locomotives go into service in France. In the next few years, steam railroads start up in Austria, Belgium, Canada, Holland, Italy, Russia, Spain, Sweden, and Switzerland.
•**1831** American Joseph Henry makes a practical electric motor that uses direct current from a battery.
•**1832** Horse-drawn streetcar services start in New York and in France.

Early screw propeller

•**1836** Screw propellers for ships are successfully tested in England by Francis Pettit Smith and by John Ericsson, a Swedish-American.
•**1837** Inventors in the UK and America develop the electric telegraph, a form of instant communication that will be widely used by railroads.
•**1838** Two ships – *Sirius* and *Great Western* – cross the Atlantic under steam power alone. Regular transatlantic passenger services soon follow.

Brunel's *Great Western*, 1837

•**1839** An 80-ft (25-m) cast-iron bridge across Dunlap's Creek in Pennsylvania is the first all-metal bridge in the US.
•**1839** Kirkpatrick Macmillan, a Scottish blacksmith, builds a pedal-powered bicycle, but the idea does not catch on. *See* MILESTONES 1885.
•**1839** A battery-powered electric paddleboat is built in Russia.

1840   1845

1840	1841	1842	1843	1844	1846	1847	1848	1849

AIR

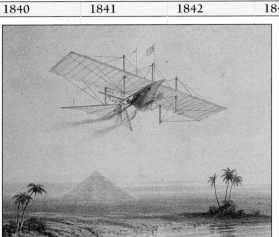

•1843 AERIAL STEAM CARRIAGE *UK*

Despite all the excitement over balloons, a few pioneers were interested in developing "heavier-than-air" flying machines, later called airplanes. William Henson showed what the future might hold when he proposed a huge Aerial Steam Carriage, designed to carry passengers from Europe to China. But with a heavy steam engine to drive its propellers, such a machine could never have left the ground.

Henson's Aerial Steam Carriage, 1843

Propeller fitted here

Stringfellow's monoplane, 1848

•1848 STEAM-POWERED MONOPLANE *UK*

It has been claimed that the first powered machine ever to fly was a 10-ft (3-m) wide steam-powered model built by John Stringfellow. This was a single-winged machine, or monoplane, with two propellers. It showed many of the important features of future aircraft. Launched from an overhead wire, the model lacked stability, and soon fell to the ground.

Housing for steam engine

Curved wing of wood and canvas

Separate tail

Chimney

Steam dome

Fuel tender

Model Norris locomotive, 1843

Bogie

Driving wheel

LAND

c.1840 PRAIRIE SCHOONER *US*

Families moving to settle in the American West made the journey in rugged, canvas-covered wagons pulled by teams of mules or oxen. From a distance, the white-topped wagons looked like sailing ships as they crossed the wide grasslands (prairies), so they were called prairie schooners. Convoys of 100 or more wagons traveled about 20 miles (30 km) a day on a trek that could take up to five months.

Prairie schooner, c.1840

•1843 LOCOMOTIVE *US*

As railroads expanded rapidly, new companies were formed to supply them with locomotives. Those built by William Norris's company in Philadelphia had their main driving wheels at the back. The front rested on a four-wheeled "bogie" that could swivel as the locomotive negotiated sharp bends.

London "knife-board" omnibus, 1847

•1847 OMNIBUS *UK*

Early London omnibuses were small because they were taxed according to the number of passengers they could carry. When the tax was abolished, buses with seats on the roof were introduced to carry more people. These double-deckers were called knife-boards because the back-to-back seats resembled a board used for cleaning knives. Passengers climbed up iron rungs to reach the top deck.

WATER

c.1840 MERCHANT BRIG *Europe*

Magnificent wooden sailing ships continued to carry their cargoes across the world's oceans throughout the 19th century, even though steamships – and ships built of iron or steel – were beginning to appear. To keep moving when the wind was very light, the crew of a two-masted "brig" might hoist more than twenty separate square or triangular sails. In strong winds most sails would be furled, or rolled up, leaving only one or two to catch the wind.

Model of a merchant brig, c.1840

Bowsprit

Extra sails were hung from small yards, and booms added to the main yards.

•1845 SAMPAN *China*

Flat bottomed wooden crafts called sampans have been widely used in China and other Eastern countries for many years. On rivers, sampans were usually rowed, but in coastal waters, one or two masts were added to carry sails. Some had a raised deck at the stern while others – like this model – carried a simple shelter "amidships" (in the middle of the boat). Sampans are still used for fishing and for carrying goods, and in overcrowded areas people even make their homes in them.

The boatman propels the sampan with a single oar.

The roofing is made of matting.

Decorated Chinese model sampan

MILESTONES

1840–1844

- **1840s** Long, low sailing ships called clippers start to be used for bringing tea to Europe and America from China.
- **1840s** Railroad signals of the semaphore (moving arm) type begin to replace flags and banners for communicating with the drivers of moving trains.
- **1840s** Large numbers of pioneers begin to migrate to the American West. Each spring, convoys of "prairie schooners" set off on the arduous trek from Independence, Missouri.
- **1841** In England, Thomas Cook runs his first "excursion," a special train from Leicester to Loughborough. The world tourist trade will grow from this small beginning.
- **1841** Rail passengers can now travel 150 miles (250 km) in less than 7 hours – three times more quickly than traveling by stagecoach.
- **1842** In France, 53 people die in the world's first major train crash, when a locomotive pulling an express train breaks one of its axles.
- **1844** An English sailor named Peter Halket makes the world's first inflatable boat out of canvas and rubber.

1845–1849

- **1845** R.W. Thompson patents his "aerial tires" in England. These air-filled, or pneumatic, tires give a comfortable ride and are used on some horse-drawn carriages.
- **1845** Brunel's iron ship *Great Britain* becomes the first propeller-driven liner to cross the Atlantic Ocean.
- **1847** In the US, an experimental electric car is built by Moses G. Farmer.

Launch of the *Great Britain*, 1845

- **1848** John Stringfellow's steam-powered model airplane is launched in England, and almost flies.
- **1848** The first railroad in South America opens, linking Georgetown and Plaisance in Guyana.
- **1849** A suspension bridge built across the Ohio River is the first to be more than 1,000 ft (300 m) long. It is supported by iron wires, but collapses in a storm a few years later.
- **1849** The Austrians send 200 pilotless hot-air balloons toward Venice. The balloons carry bombs, but the "air raid" fails because the wind changes direction.

1850

Poitevin's equestrian ascent, 1850

•1850
HORSEBACK BALLOON *France*

As the public lost interest in ordinary balloon flights, some balloonists tried more risky feats. One stunt was to fly aloft with animals – or even riding on their backs. The French balloonist Poitevin took off on his pony *Blanche* from the Paris Hippodrome in 1850. There were protests against the cruelty of such flights. In fact, on a visit to England in 1852, the courts banned Poitevin's wife from making an ascent on a bull!

•1852
STEAM AIRSHIP *France*

In 1852, a French engineer named Henri Giffard designed a dirigible powered by a 3 hp (2.25 kW) steam engine that turned a propeller 11 ft (3.4 m) in diameter. On September 24, 1852, Giffard, dressed in top hat and frock coat, piloted his airship on a 17-mile (27-km) journey from the center of Paris. Although Giffard's airship only traveled at 6 mph (10 kph), it was the first successful powered flight ever made.

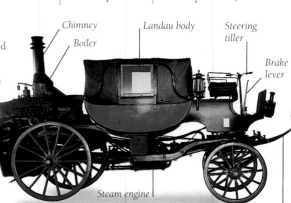

Steering rudder

Landing ropes to tie down airship

Model of Giffard's airship, 1852

•1850 HORSE-POWERED LOCOMOTIVE *Germany*

Steam locomotives were expensive to buy and run, so on small railroad lines horses continued to pull trains. Enthusiastic inventors tried to find alternatives to the steam locomotive. Some devised "atmospheric" railroads, for example, using air pressure to push the trains along. Others built curious locomotives that were powered by horses walking on a moving belt. But nothing could compete with the increasing speed and power of steam locomotives.

Horse-powered locomotive, 1850

Elephant with howdah, 1852

•1852 ELEPHANT *India*

From a covered seat, or howdah, fixed to an elephant's back, Indian royalty had a superb all-around view when they went hunting. As the elephant crossed rugged country and even rivers, the hunters sat above in comfort and safety. *See* **ARMORED ELEPHANT c.1600**.

•1854
STEAM CARRIAGE *Italy*

Engineers in several countries dreamed of steam vehicles that would rival horse-drawn stagecoaches. A number of carriages were made, including one built in Turin, Italy, by Virgilio Bordino, an Italian army engineer. Bordino's vehicle achieved 5 mph (8 kph) on a level road. It used the body of a landau, a popular horse-drawn carriage of the time.

Chimney — *Landau body* — *Steering tiller*

Boiler

Brake lever

Steam engine

Bordino's steam carriage, 1854

Towing bar

Sail of matted palm leaves

Whaling scene, 1855

Model of an Indonesian boat used to hunt sperm whales

Harpoon

Paddle

Eye for the boat to see with

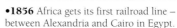

•1855
WHALING SHIPS

For hundreds of years, local sailors throughout the world hunted whales for meat. This Indonesian boat was used to hunt whales three times its own size. In the 19th century, the demand for whale products in Europe and North America was so great that thousands of whales were slaughtered every year. Whales were killed by harpoons thrown from rowboats, and then towed back to a larger ship, a "whaler," where oil and other products were extracted.

•1858
GREAT EASTERN *UK*

Designed by the British engineer Isambard Brunel, the *Great Eastern* had many innovations. More than 650 ft (200 m) long, its hull was made of two layers of iron plates. It had five masts to carry sails, but was also powered by steam, with a four-bladed propeller as well as two paddle wheels. *Great Eastern* was a technical success and made 11 transatlantic trips, but it could not attract enough passengers to run at a profit.

Model of *Great Eastern*, 1858

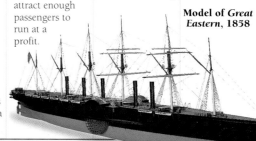

•**1850s** Railroad networks expand rapidly. There are now 9,000 miles (14,500 km) of track in the US, and 6,100 miles (9,800 km) in the UK. Railroads begin to take over from canals as a means of transporting goods.

•**1850** The development of modern skiing begins when a Norwegian, Sondre Norheim, devises stiffer bindings to attach skis to boots. Loose-bound skis were used for thousands of years in northern Europe and Asia.

•**1852** Henri Giffard's steam-powered airship flies in France.

•**1853** In England, Sir George Cayley builds and tests a person-carrying glider.

•**1853** The first railroad in Asia is opened, between Bombay and Thana in India. In the following year, railroads will also open in Australia and Brazil.

•**1854** In New York, Eli Otis demonstrates an elevator, or "lift," with a safety device to stop it from plunging to the ground if the cable breaks. As taller buildings are built, Otis elevators will become well known around the world.

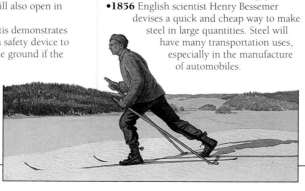

Cross-country skiing, Norway

•**1856** Africa gets its first railroad line – between Alexandria and Cairo in Egypt.

•**1856** English scientist Henry Bessemer devises a quick and cheap way to make steel in large quantities. Steel will have many transportation uses, especially in the manufacture of automobiles.

•**1858** Australia's first balloon ascent is made by William Dean in Melbourne.

•**1859** Edwin L. Drake drills the first successful oil well, at Titusville in Pennsylvania. This is the start of a vast oil and gas industry that will supply essential fuel for transportation in the 20th century.

•**1859** The French warship *La Gloire* is the first "iron-clad" – a wooden ship with a hull protected by a layer of iron plates.

•**1859** In France, Étienne Lenoir develops the first reliable internal combustion engine, running on coal gas. By the early part of the 20th century, this new type of engine will have revolutionized the world of transportation.

1860   1865

1860	1861	1862	1863	1864	1865	1866	1867	1868	1869

AIR

•1863 STEAM HELICOPTER *France*
In the 15th century, the Italian artist and thinker Leonardo da Vinci sketched a simple helicopter to be lifted by a single rotating spiral wing, or "rotor." In the 19th century, Sir George Cayley (*see* **MILESTONES 1853**) and other flight pioneers built a number of successful model helicopters, each of which was lifted by a rotor with several blades. These, and news of Giffard's airship (*see* **STEAM AIRSHIP 1852**), may have inspired the inventor Gabriel de la Landelle to design his fantastic Steam Airliner. It was never built, and could never have flown.

Gabriel de la Landelle's Steam Airliner

•1868 GLIDER *France*
A bold attempt at practical flying was made by a French sea captain, Jean-Marie le Bris, when he tried out two full-size gliders. Their design was based on the shape of an albatross, a seabird with a huge wingspan that Le Bris had studied on a visit to South America. The gliders were launched from a moving cart and probably had an adjustable tail and wings. Both gliders crashed after a few short trial flights.

Le Bris's glider, 1868

Compartment for driver

Water tank

Pipe taking steam and smoke to water tanks

Underground railroad locomotive, 1866

LAND

•1860 HORSE-DRAWN STREETCAR *US/Europe*
Streetcars running on metal rails embedded in the streets were widely used in American and European cities in the 1860s. Horses could pull many more passengers in a vehicle on smooth rails than in a bus on uneven roads. This gave the passengers a cheaper, faster, and more comfortable ride.

Horse-drawn streetcar, London, England, 1860

•1863 UNDERGROUND RAILROAD *England*
As cities grew larger, their streets became choked with horse-drawn traffic. To ease the problem in London, a railroad was built beneath the city's streets. Called the Metropolitan, it was the world's first underground railroad. People flocked to use it, even though the smoke from the steam locomotives pulling the trains made it smelly and dirty.

•1869 SLED *Arctic lands*
The lands within the Arctic Circle are covered with snow and ice for much of the year, so sturdy, thick-coated husky dogs were specially bred for pulling sleds. When harnessed to a strong sled, a team of eight huskies can pull up to a 0.5 ton of cargo. Antarctic explorers used dog sleds when they searched for the South Pole.

Painting of Inuit sled, 1869

WATER

•1860 IRON WARSHIP *UK*
War at sea moved into a new era when navies replaced their wooden ships with iron ones, which were less likely to catch fire in battle. HMS *Warrior* was the first warship built entirely of iron. This 40-gun ship could do 15 knots (17 mph/28 kph) under steam, but also carried a full set of sails. To protect it from the guns of enemy ships, *Warrior's* hull was armored with iron plates 4.5 in (11 cm) thick.

Model of HMS *Warrior*, 1860

•1868 CLIPPER SHIPS *US/UK*
Clippers were sleek merchant vessels designed for speed rather than carrying large cargoes. Some clippers averaged 20 knots (23 mph/37 kph) for hours on end. The fastest clipper was the British ship *Thermopylae*, launched in 1868. The American clipper *Great Republic* was the largest wooden sailing ship ever built. Clippers carried cargo and passengers from New York to San Francisco during California's gold rush of 1849. They raced to bring tea from China in the 1860s and wool from Australia in the 1880s.

The American clipper ship *Great Republic*, 1853–72

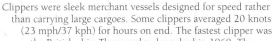

MILESTONES

1860–1864
•**1860** HMS *Warrior*, the first iron warship, is launched in the UK.
•**1860** The Pony Express mail service starts in the US. Letters now reach California from Missouri in only ten days.
•**1861** In France, Ernest Michaux makes a bicycle, or "vélocipède," with pedals at the front that riders turn with their feet.
•**1862** French engineer Alphonse Beau de Rochas patents the four-stroke cycle for internal combustion engines. Nikolaus Otto, a German, will build the first one in 1876.

•**1863** The world's first underground railroad is opened in London, England.
•**1863** In the US, James Plimpton designs roller skates that allow the wearer to turn corners.
•**1863** Englishman Thomas Weston patents the friction clutch, a device that connects an engine to its gears and wheels.
•**1864** American George Pullman designs a railroad sleeping car with bunk beds. Luxurious "Pullman Cars" will run on many routes in North America and Europe.

The US is crossed by rail, 1869

1865–1869
•**1865** A British law limits self-propelled road vehicles to 4 mph (6 kph). They must have a man with a red flag walking 180 ft (55 m) ahead.
•**1867** Joseph Monier in France embeds metal rods in wet concrete to make "reinforced concrete."
•**1867** Frenchman L.G. Perreaux creates the first motorcycle when he fits a steam engine to Michaux's vélocipède. *See* **MILESTONES 1861**
•**1869** The 100-mile (160-km) Suez Canal opens, linking the Mediterranean to the Red Sea.

•**1869** A coast-to-coast railroad is completed in the US when the Central Pacific and Union Pacific Railroads meet near Great Salt Lake.
•**1869** The first cog, or "rack-and-pinion," railroad opens on the slopes of Mt. Washington, New Hampshire. The locomotive has a gear wheel that meshes with a toothed rack between the rails so it does not slip.
•**1869** American engineer George Westinghouse patents a braking system worked by compressed air.

1870

1875

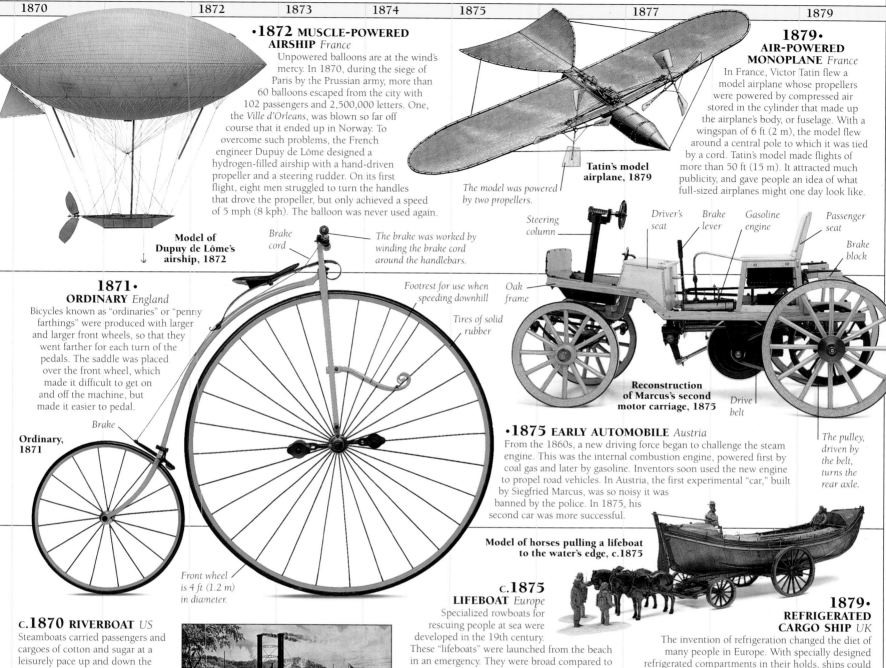

•1872 MUSCLE-POWERED AIRSHIP *France*

Unpowered balloons are at the wind's mercy. In 1870, during the siege of Paris by the Prussian army, more than 60 balloons escaped from the city with 102 passengers and 2,500,000 letters. One, the *Ville d'Orleans*, was blown so far off course that it ended up in Norway. To overcome such problems, the French engineer Dupuy de Lôme designed a hydrogen-filled airship with a hand-driven propeller and a steering rudder. On its first flight, eight men struggled to turn the handles that drove the propeller, but only achieved a speed of 5 mph (8 kph). The balloon was never used again.

Model of Dupuy de Lôme's airship, 1872 ↓

1879• AIR-POWERED MONOPLANE *France*

In France, Victor Tatin flew a model airplane whose propellers were powered by compressed air stored in the cylinder that made up the airplane's body, or fuselage. With a wingspan of 6 ft (2 m), the model flew around a central pole to which it was tied by a cord. Tatin's model made flights of more than 50 ft (15 m). It attracted much publicity, and gave people an idea of what full-sized airplanes might one day look like.

Tatin's model airplane, 1879

The model was powered by two propellers.

Steering column

Driver's seat — *Brake lever* — *Gasoline engine* — *Passenger seat*

Brake block

Oak frame

1871• ORDINARY *England*

Bicycles known as "ordinaries" or "penny farthings" were produced with larger and larger front wheels, so that they went farther for each turn of the pedals. The saddle was placed over the front wheel, which made it difficult to get on and off the machine, but made it easier to pedal.

Ordinary, 1871

Brake

Brake cord

The brake was worked by winding the brake cord around the handlebars.

Footrest for use when speeding downhill

Tires of solid rubber

Reconstruction of Marcus's second motor carriage, 1875

Drive belt

The pulley, driven by the belt, turns the rear axle.

•1875 EARLY AUTOMOBILE *Austria*

From the 1860s, a new driving force began to challenge the steam engine. This was the internal combustion engine, powered first by coal gas and later by gasoline. Inventors soon used the new engine to propel road vehicles. In Austria, the first experimental "car," built by Siegfried Marcus, was so noisy it was banned by the police. In 1875, his second car was more successful.

Front wheel is 4 ft (1.2 m) in diameter.

c.1870 RIVERBOAT *US*

Steamboats carried passengers and cargoes of cotton and sugar at a leisurely pace up and down the Mississippi River. The river is very shallow in places, so they were built as flat-bottomed paddle steamers, with the engines and several decks above the waterline. Passenger riverboats were often luxurious, with fine carpets, chandeliers, and music provided by an orchestra.

Mississippi paddle steamer, c.1870

Model of horses pulling a lifeboat to the water's edge, c.1875

c.1875 LIFEBOAT *Europe*

Specialized rowboats for rescuing people at sea were developed in the 19th century. These "lifeboats" were launched from the beach in an emergency. They were broad compared to their length to make them less likely to capsize. To help them float even when filled with water, they had cork attached around the sides or air-filled chambers. Some were even "self-righting," so that they returned the right way up after capsizing.

***Orient* refrigerated cargo ship, 1879**

1879• REFRIGERATED CARGO SHIP *UK*

The invention of refrigeration changed the diet of many people in Europe. With specially designed refrigerated compartments in their holds, ships could bring meat from as far away as America and Australia without it rotting. Because the meat came from vast herds and flocks kept on huge ranches, it was much cheaper than European beef and lamb.

•**1870s** Elevated railroads go into service in several cities in the US and Europe. Running above the streets, they are cheaper to build than underground railroads.

•**1870s** Nearly 25 million Europeans will buy a one-way ticket across the Atlantic in the next 50 years. They are emigrants seeking a new life in North America. Most travel "steerage," the cheapest class on a boat.

•**1871** The first wind tunnel is built in England. Wind tunnels will be used to test the design of cars and airplanes by blowing air past a stationary model.

•**1872** The first railroad in Japan opens, linking Tokyo to Yokohama. Japan's first steam riverboat service also starts this year.

•**1872** Thousands of the horses that pull city streetcars in the US catch a serious infectious illness, paralyzing public transportation.

•**1873** Cable streetcars start to run in San Francisco, California. They are pulled along by gripping a moving cable underneath the track.

•**1874** The first bridge to be made partly of steel is built across the Mississippi River.

The *Zenith* balloon tragedy, 1875

•**1875** Siegfried Marcus tries out a gasoline-driven road vehicle in Vienna.

•**1875** Work starts on a tunnel to link England and France under the English Channel. It will be halted by fears that England might be invaded through the tunnel, as will an attempt in 1882.

•**1875** Three Frenchmen reach a record height of 5.3 miles (8.6 km) in the *Zenith* balloon, but two die from cold and asphyxiation.

•**1877** The British navy launches the first steel warship, HMS *Iris*.

•**1877** A steamship, the *Paraguay*, carries the first cargo of frozen meat from Argentina to Europe.

•**1877** A wrought-iron cantilever bridge across the Kentucky River is the first of its type in the US. Cantilevers have arms built out from each side that touch in the middle.

•**1878** The world's first oil tanker comes into service on the Caspian Sea between Iran and Russia.

•**1879** The first electric railroad is built by the engineer Werner von Siemens, and runs at 4 mph (6 kph) at an exhibition in Berlin, Germany.

1880–1959 Powered flight and the rise of the automobile

Assembly-line production of Model T Fords, 1913

IN 1880 THERE WERE NO CARS in the world. Eighty years later, there were 95 million of them, all powered by gasoline-driven internal combustion engines that were faster, lighter, and more powerful than the old steam engines. The internal combustion engine also transformed air and sea travel, and dramatically shaped the course of the 20th century.

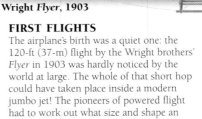

Prototypes of the Volkswagen Beetle, 1936

CARS FOR THE MASSES

Early, hand-built cars such as the Rolls-Royce Silver Ghost were hugely expensive. A new way of manufacturing called mass production changed the history of the car. Cars mass-produced on factory assembly lines, such as the Ford Model T and the Volkswagen Beetle, became cheap enough for ordinary people to afford. Improved roads and specially built intercity roads made cars a very convenient way to travel.

The gasoline engine rings the changes

More than anything else, cars gave their owners the freedom to go where they wanted, when they wanted. With their new mobility, car owners could choose to live far away from where they worked, in areas known as "suburbs" on the outskirts of cities. People who could not afford cars relied mainly on public transportation. The early years of the 20th century were a golden age for railroads, and on city streets efficient streetcars and buses put horse-drawn vehicles out of business. On water, the diesel engine – a type of internal combustion engine – was put to work on smaller vessels, while bigger ships were driven by steam turbines. The age of large sailing ships was virtually at an end.

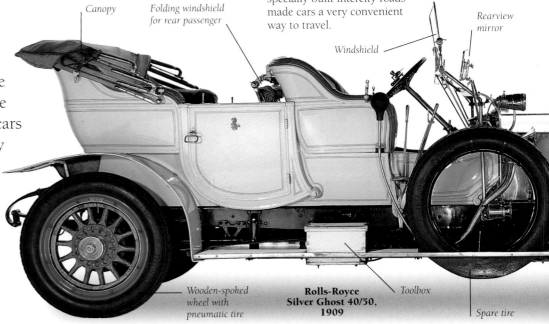

Canopy
Folding windshield for rear passenger
Windshield
Rearview mirror
Wooden-spoked wheel with pneumatic tire
Rolls-Royce Silver Ghost 40/50, 1909
Toolbox
Spare tire

THE CHANGING WORLD: 1880–1959

The world's first public electric railroad, Lichterfelde, Germany, 1881

ELECTRIC POWER
Electric-powered public transportation systems saved the fast-growing cities of the early 20th century from chaos. Taking power from an overhead cable or extra ground rail, electric trains and streetcars had good acceleration and could stop quickly. Electricity is efficient and pollution-free, but dirty fuels such as coal and oil were still being burned in power stations to generate the electricity.

THE OIL BONANZA
After 1900, petroleum oil began to replace coal as transportation's main energy source. Fuels made from this thick, black liquid pack maximum energy into minimum weight and space. Oil, or "liquid gold" as it has been called, is the decomposed remains of marine creatures that lived millions of years ago. It is found in underground reservoirs, and has to be pumped to the surface at oil wells. Oil wells were first established in the US, and later in Russia, the Middle East, and elsewhere.

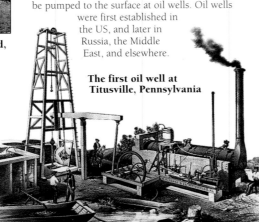

The first oil well at Titusville, Pennsylvania

Wright *Flyer*, 1903

FIRST FLIGHTS
The airplane's birth was a quiet one: the 120-ft (37-m) flight by the Wright brothers' *Flyer* in 1903 was hardly noticed by the world at large. The whole of that short hop could have taken place inside a modern jumbo jet! The pioneers of powered flight had to work out what size and shape an airplane should be, and how to control it. The Wrights used "wing-warping," gentle twisting of the wings, to control the *Flyer*. Later airplanes used hinged wing-flaps called ailerons to achieve the same effect.

FLOATING HOTELS
Getting there was more than half the fun in the age of the luxury ocean liner. In the years before World War II, liners grew in size, speed, and comfort, carrying hundreds of wealthy passengers in conditions of the utmost grandeur and elegance. They traveled at a pace that seems relaxed by modern standards – a journey from Europe to America, for example, took four or five days.

The dining room of a luxury liner, c.1910

Opening of a new motorway, or autobahn, in Germany, 1935

The dawn of the air age

The lightweight internal combustion engine at last made airplanes a practical reality. Unlike balloons, the new flying machines could stay aloft even though they were heavier than the air they moved through. Like ballooning a century before, "heavier-than-air" flying was something early enthusiasts did mainly for fun. Only when airplanes were used for military purposes during World War I did people begin to take them seriously. Passenger services began to be available in the 1920s, although air travel was still slow and arduous by modern standards. By the 1950s, the first jet airliners were carrying passengers swiftly and comfortably between continents. The pace of development had been so rapid that many people who watched these jets flying overhead could remember a time when there had been no airplanes or even cars.

A world divided

Despite the speed and excitement of new forms of transportation, the freedom to travel was mostly limited to people in the industrialized countries of North America and Europe. In 1914, for example, the average person in the US traveled about 1,600 miles (2,500 km) each year, most of it on foot. Fifty years later, they went twice as far each month, mainly by car. In the less developed world, most people were still walking everywhere in 1960.

The distinctive "Spirit of Ecstasy" mascot was added in 1911.

TRANSPORTATION TECHNOLOGY

WINGS – THE SECRET OF POWERED FLIGHT

The top surface of an aircraft wing bulges upward, while the underside is nearly flat. As an aircraft moves forward, its wing cuts through the air. Some air flows smoothly over the wing, speeding up as it travels over the curved surface; some passes below the wing, with its speed unchanged. Fast-moving air exerts less pressure than slow-moving air, so the downward pressure above the wing is less than the upward pressure below it. The result is an upward force called lift that keeps the aircraft aloft. The faster the aircraft goes, the stronger the lift.

Slow-moving air exerts strong upward pressure

Avro triplane IV, 1910

Fast-moving air exerts weaker downward pressure

INTERNAL COMBUSTION

Setting off explosions inside a metal tube seems an unlikely way to power cars, ships, or aircraft – but it works! In most internal combustion engines, a spark ignites a mixture of air and gasoline vapor inside a cylinder. The resulting explosion pushes out a piston, whose motion is used to rotate a crank that turns the engine. As the piston falls back, the burned gas is forced out of the cylinder and a new charge of air and fuel is drawn in for the next explosion. Most engines have at least four cylinders that fire in turn. A diesel engine compresses the air and fuel mixture so much that it explodes of its own accord.

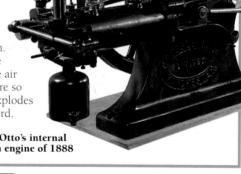

Nikolaus Otto's internal combustion engine of 1888

FARM MACHINERY

The internal combustion engine transformed farming, just as it did many other areas of life. In the 1900s, gasoline-powered tractors began to replace draft animals for pulling plows and other machinery. By 1950, there were 4 million tractors in the US and 2 million in the rest of the world. Trucks made it easier for farmers to take produce and animals to market, while self-propelled combine harvesters enabled grain to be harvested more quickly.

Advertisement for Glasgow tractor, 1919

THE GOLDEN AGE OF RAILROADS

For intercity travel, the railroads reigned supreme. Fierce competition between rival companies meant that standards of service were higher during the early part of the 20th century than ever before or since. Stations and railroad hotels were often grand establishments, and of great architectural merit. By 1960, railroads were past their peak in the main industrialized countries, although they were still growing elsewhere.

Grand Central Station, New York, 1913

RECREATION AND SPORTS

Growing interest in sports and leisure activities promoted improvements in the technology of transportation. Waterskiing and surfing, for example, led to the development of new materials from which to make tougher, longer-lasting skis and surfboards. Similarly, the tough demands of long-distance road races helped car makers know which parts were most likely to break. They could then build more reliable vehicles for general sale.

Waterskiing in the US, 1920s

WAR AND PEACE

During the two World Wars (1914–18 and 1939–45), military forces needed to deliver weapons, troops, and materials rapidly to battle zones. This brought great advances in the technology and design of ships, airplanes, and land vehicles. As soon as peace returned, these advances were put to civilian use. For example, work in Germany on liquid-fueled rockets in the 1940s led directly to American successes in space two decades later.

British Mountain Howitzer gun, World War II

1880

1885

| 1880 | 1881 | 1882 | 1883 | 1884 | 1885 | 1886 | | 1889 |

AIR

The hydrogen-filled gas bag was 92 ft (28 m) long.

•1883–84 ELECTRIC-POWERED AIRSHIPS *France*

In their search for a power source to drive an airship, French aeronauts turned to the electric motor. The brothers Gaston and Albert Tissandier built a balloon big enough to lift heavy batteries, a motor, and passengers, but it only crawled through the air at less than 3 mph (5 kph). Charles Renard and Arthur Krebs built an even larger balloon, *La France*. Its batteries and motor weighed nearly 1 ton, but it managed a speed of 14 mph (23 kph). In a moderate or strong wind, even *La France* could make no headway.

La France, 1884 Powered by an electric motor, it was the first fully controllable airship.

A rudder in the form of a sail was used to guide the airship.

Model of the Tissandiers' airship, 1883

The car was suspended by rigging from a "jacket" around the gas bag.

Brake lever

Tank containing water to cool the engine.

Tangent-spoked wire wheel

LAND

c.1880 TRAVOIS *North America*

The North American Indian peoples carried their belongings on a simple vehicle called a travois, made from two long poles pulled by a dog or horse. The travois has a long history, and may have been used in some parts of the world even earlier than the sled. *See* SLED **5000 BC**.

Plains Indians with travois, 1880

1886•
BENZ MOTOR CAR *Germany*

A gasoline-driven three-wheeler built by Karl Benz in 1885 can probably be called the world's first true automobile. When Benz showed it in public the following year, the two-seater "Motorwagen" reached a speed of 8 mph (13 kph). The engine was mounted under the passenger seat, and drove the rear wheels by means of a moving belt. Benz set up the first factory to produce three-wheeled and later four-wheeled cars. The car industry grew from these small beginnings.

1885•
DAIMLER MOTORCYCLE *Germany*

A vital step in the development of the automobile came when the German engineer Gottfried Daimler built a gasoline engine that turned three times faster than any existing engine. He fixed one of these compact, high-speed engines to a wooden-wheeled bicycle. In 1886, Daimler made a four-wheeled vehicle by attaching an engine to a carriage.

Replica of Daimler motorcycle, 1885

Metal-rimmed wooden wheel

Solid rubber tires

Benz Motorwagen, 1886

WATER

Servia, the all-steel cargo ship, 1881

1881•
STEEL CARGO LINER *UK*

The invention of a new and more reliable way of making steel – the Siemens process – meant that ships no longer had to be built of iron. Steel plates were lighter than iron ones, and could be made thinner but just as strong. *Servia* was the first all-steel cargo ship. It also carried passengers, and was the first ship to have electric lights in its public rooms.

The guns had swiveling mountings so they could fire in several directions.

•1888
STEEL WARSHIP *Japan*

By the late 19th century, navies around the world were strengthening and modernizing their fleets. As Japan emerged as a military and industrial power, its Imperial Navy acquired many new vessels. One of them, the cruiser *Takao*, was the first steel ship built in Japan. Faster and lighter than battleships, cruisers carried guns but were not protected with armor-plating.

Model of Takao, 1888

MILESTONES

1880–1884

- **1880** China's first permanent railroad opens.
- **1881** In Germany, the world's first public electric railroad opens at Lichterfelde, near Berlin. It is 1.5 miles (2.5 km) long.
- **1882** The 9-mile (15-km) St. Gotthard rail tunnel under the Alps is completed, linking Italy and Switzerland.
- **1882** In Germany, the engineers Gottfried Daimler and Wilhelm Maybach start to develop high-speed gasoline engines.

- **1883** The world's longest suspension bridge, the Brooklyn Bridge, opens in New York.
- **1883** The luxurious *Orient Express* rail service carries its first passengers. It runs between Paris, in France, and Constantinople (now Istanbul), in Turkey.
- **1884** British engineer Sir Charles Parsons patents the steam turbine, a form of high-speed steam engine.
- **1884** The first practical airship, *La France*, flies in Paris, powered by a large, electrically driven propeller.

DINING SALOON
GNR

Luxury rail travel in the late 19th century

1885–1889

- **1885** The first specially built oil tanker, the *Glückauf*, is built at Newcastle, England.
- **1885** Karl Benz, a German engineer, builds his gasoline-powered "Motorwagen" – the world's first true car.
- **1885** In England, J.K. Starley's "Rover" safety bicycle is the first to use the classic design of two equal-sized wheels, the rear one driven by a chain from the pedals.
- **1886** The first successful tandem bicycles (carrying two people, one behind the other) are built in the UK, and soon become popular.

Dunlop's pneumatic tires on his son's bicycle

- **1886** The Canadian Pacific Railroad's transcontinental route is completed, with a total length of 2,880 miles (4,635 km).
- **1888** Scotsman John B. Dunlop reinvents the air-filled, or pneumatic, tire (*see* MILESTONES **1845**) for use in his son's bicycle. Pneumatic tires will soon become standard on all cars and bicycles.
- **1889** After a major rail crash, automatic brakes are made compulsory on British trains.
- **1889** A steam locomotive reaches 89 mph (143 kph) on the Paris–Dijon line in France.

1895

The high wings had a frame like the skeleton of a bat's wing.

•1890
ADER'S ÉOLE *France*
The engineer Clément Ader devised a lightweight but powerful steam engine and fitted it to his bat-winged monoplane *Éole*. With its inventor aboard, *Éole* took off under its own power from a level surface at Armainvilliers, France. It was more of a hop than a flight, but *Éole* still managed to skim along close to the ground for about 165 ft (50 m).

— *Steering column*

Model of Ader's *Éole*, 1891

Éole's steam engine drove a single propeller with four blades.

•1895
GLIDER *Germany*
Launching himself into the wind from suitable high places, Otto Lilienthal made many flights in a range of gliders that he designed and built himself. In his No. 11 glider, he flew a distance of 1,150 ft (350 m), controlling the flight by changing the position of his body, like a modern hang glider. He died when one of his gliders crashed in 1896. His flights probably inspired the Wright brothers. See **WRIGHT FLYER 1903**.

Lilienthal could control the glider by swinging his legs and changing its center of gravity.

Reconstruction of Lilienthal's No. 11 glider, 1895

Cotton wing cover supported by willow ribs

Japanese jinrikisha, 1892

1892•
JINRIKISHA *Japan*
A "human horse" ran between the shafts of the jinrikisha, a sort of taxi-cart popular in the cities of Japan and other Asian countries at the end of the 19th century. The runners pulled their "rickshaws," as they were called by European tourists, as far as 30 miles (48 km) in one day. The jinrikisha was banned in many cities because people felt it was wrong to use people like animals.

•1895
ELECTRIC LOCOMOTIVE *US*
The first mainline railroad to use electric trains was the Baltimore and Ohio in the US. Four miles (6.5 km) of track that ran largely in tunnels were converted to electric power because smoke from steam locomotives was a nuisance. The trains were hauled by electric locomotives, which drew their current from a rigid rail running overhead.

B&O electric locomotive with overhead power rail

•1897 STEAM CAR *US*
In the early days of driving, steam cars and gasoline cars were rivals. In Massachusetts, the Stanley brothers built a successful steam car that went into commercial production under the name Locomobile. Although it used 1 gallon (4.5 liters) of water every mile and took 30 minutes to get up steam on a cold morning, the Locomobile was so popular that more than 5,000 were sold.

The Stanley Locomobile steam car

1895•
ROYAL BARGE *Burma*
Since ancient times, royalty have liked to ride in fine barges on ceremonial occasions. This royal barge was used on the Irrawaddy River by the King of Burma, who sat in the raised area in the middle. It was richly decorated, to remind people of his power and wealth, and rowed by oarsmen in colorful costumes.

Model of Burmese Royal Barge, 1895

•1897 *TURBINIA* UK
A new era began when Charles Parsons's ship *Turbinia* achieved the astonishing speed of 34.5 knots (40 mph/64 kph) thanks to a special type of engine called a steam turbine. Lighter than ordinary steam engines, the turbine used a jet of steam to turn a set of blades attached to the propeller shaft.

Turbinia, 1897

•**1890** The world's first electric "tube" railroad opens in London, England. It runs inside a tunnel bored deep under the Thames River.
•**1890** In France, Clément Ader's *Éole* is the first full-sized, person-carrying airplane to take off under its own power.
•**1890** In Scotland, the massive Forth railroad bridge is completed.
•**1891** Frenchmen Emile Levassor and René Panhard design the first car to have its engine at the front, driving the rear wheels through a clutch and gearbox.

•**1891** In Germany, Otto Lilienthal makes the first of a series of experimental glider flights.
•**1892** The escalator is invented by Jesse Reno in the US.
•**1892** In Germany, Rudolph Diesel patents a new internal combustion engine. Diesel engines will become standard for all heavy road vehicles.
•**1893** The Duryea brothers of Springfield, Massachusetts, build the US's first successful gasoline car.
•**1893** Australian Lawrence Hargrave invents the box kite, which will influence later airplane designers.

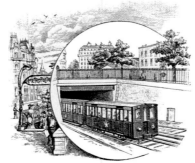

The Paris Métro

•**1895** The Kiel Canal is completed in Germany, providing a shipping route between the Baltic and North seas.
•**1895** The world's first official road race for cars takes place in France, from Paris to Bordeaux and back.
•**1895** A mainline electric railroad service starts on a stretch of the Baltimore and Ohio Railroad.
•**1896** Britain's Red Flag Act is repealed, allowing vehicles a top speed of 12 mph (19 kph). See **MILESTONES 1865**.

•**1897** The first Stanley steam car is made in the US.
•**1897** With the success of Charles Parsons's turbine-driven *Turbinia*, steam turbines begin to be adopted for most ships.
•**1898** In Paris, France, work starts on an underground railroad system, or "Métro." It will open in 1900.
•**1899** Camille Jenatzy, a Belgian, sets a world speed record of 66 mph (106 mph) in an electric car.

1900

1905

| 1900 | 1901 | 1903 | 1904 | 1905 | 1906 | 1907 | 1908 | 1909 |

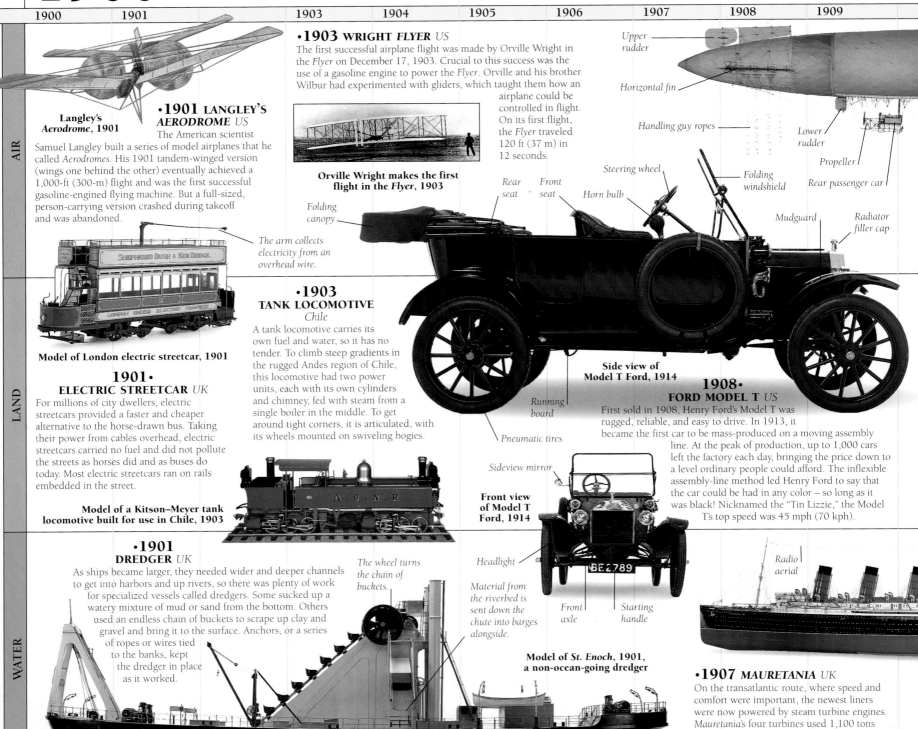

AIR

•1901 LANGLEY'S AERODROME US

Langley's Aerodrome, 1901

The American scientist Samuel Langley built a series of model airplanes that he called *Aerodromes*. His 1901 tandem-winged version (wings one behind the other) eventually achieved a 1,000-ft (300-m) flight and was the first successful gasoline-engined flying machine. But a full-sized, person-carrying version crashed during takeoff and was abandoned.

•1903 WRIGHT *FLYER* US

The first successful airplane flight was made by Orville Wright in the *Flyer* on December 17, 1903. Crucial to this success was the use of a gasoline engine to power the *Flyer*. Orville and his brother Wilbur had experimented with gliders, which taught them how an airplane could be controlled in flight. On its first flight, the *Flyer* traveled 120 ft (37 m) in 12 seconds.

Orville Wright makes the first flight in the *Flyer*, 1903

Upper rudder
Horizontal fin
Handling guy ropes
Lower rudder
Propeller
Rear passenger car

LAND

Model of London electric streetcar, 1901

The arm collects electricity from an overhead wire.

1901• ELECTRIC STREETCAR UK

For millions of city dwellers, electric streetcars provided a faster and cheaper alternative to the horse-drawn bus. Taking their power from cables overhead, electric streetcars carried no fuel and did not pollute the streets as horses did and as buses do today. Most electric streetcars ran on rails embedded in the street.

•1903 TANK LOCOMOTIVE *Chile*

A tank locomotive carries its own fuel and water, so it has no tender. To climb steep gradients in the rugged Andes region of Chile, this locomotive had two power units, each with its own cylinders and chimney, fed with steam from a single boiler in the middle. To get around tight corners, it is articulated, with its wheels mounted on swiveling bogies.

Model of a Kitson–Meyer tank locomotive built for use in Chile, 1903

Folding canopy
Rear seat
Front seat
Horn bulb
Steering wheel
Folding windshield
Mudguard
Radiator filler cap

Side view of Model T Ford, 1914

Running board
Pneumatic tires

1908• FORD MODEL T US

First sold in 1908, Henry Ford's Model T was rugged, reliable, and easy to drive. In 1913, it became the first car to be mass-produced on a moving assembly line. At the peak of production, up to 1,000 cars left the factory each day, bringing the price down to a level ordinary people could afford. The inflexible assembly-line method led Henry Ford to say that the car could be had in any color – so long as it was black! Nicknamed the "Tin Lizzie," the Model T's top speed was 45 mph (70 kph).

Sideview mirror
Headlight
Material from the riverbed is sent down the chute into barges alongside.
Front axle
Starting handle

Front view of Model T Ford, 1914

WATER

•1901 DREDGER UK

As ships became larger, they needed wider and deeper channels to get into harbors and up rivers, so there was plenty of work for specialized vessels called dredgers. Some sucked up a watery mixture of mud or sand from the bottom. Others used an endless chain of buckets to scrape up clay and gravel and bring it to the surface. Anchors, or a series of ropes or wires tied to the banks, kept the dredger in place as it worked.

The wheel turns the chain of buckets.

Model of *St. Enoch*, 1901, a non-ocean-going dredger

Radio aerial

•1907 *MAURETANIA* UK

On the transatlantic route, where speed and comfort were important, the newest liners were now powered by steam turbine engines. *Mauretania*'s four turbines used 1,100 tons (1,000 tonnes) of coal a day to go from Liverpool, England, to New York in less than five days. *Mauretania* was the first ship to use a radio receiver to take navigational bearings.

MILESTONES

| 1900–1904 | 1905–1909 |

Mechanism to raise or lower the chain of buckets as the tide changes

•**1900** Battery-powered "electric broughams," named after a horse-drawn carriage, will be popular in the US as personal transportation for the next 20 years.

•**1900** In Germany, Count Ferdinand von Zeppelin tries out the first of his enormous rigid airships. His company will build more than 100 "Zeppelins" over the next 30 years.

•**1901** In France, the Werner brothers design a motorcycle with the engine where the pedals are on a normal bicycle. This will become the standard design for all motorcycles.

•**1901** A commercial monorail, a railroad with only one rail, starts at Wuppertal, Germany. Its electric trains hang from a single, elevated rail.

•**1901** In the US, Ransom Olds uses mass-production methods in his automobile factory. It will soon make 5,000 "Oldsmobiles" a year.

•**1903** Orville Wright makes his historic first flight at Kitty Hawk, North Carolina.

•**1904** A French engineer, Eugène Freysinnet, invents "pre-stressed concrete," which will be essential for building bridges later this century.

•**1905** Motor buses appear in New York and in London, England, where they will completely replace horse-drawn buses by 1914.

Blériot's cross-Channel flight, 1909

•**1907** The luxury turbine-powered British liner *Lusitania* (sister ship of the *Mauretania*) enters service. It is the largest and fastest afloat, but will be sunk by a German submarine in 1915.

•**1907** The first successful airplane flight in Europe is made by the English-born, French-speaking Henri Farman in his *Voisin-Farman 1*. The flight lasts just over one minute.

•**1908** The Ford Motor Company introduces its Model T car. It will sell 16.5 million by 1927.

•**1908** Thérèse Peltier is the first woman to fly in an airplane.

•**1909** Louis Blériot makes the first airplane flight across the English Channel in his Type XI monoplane, winning a prize of £1,000.

1910

1915

LVG C.VI, 1917

Model of
Schütte-Lanz
SL1 rigid
airship, 1911

Nose

•1911 RIGID AIRSHIP
Germany

*Forward
passenger car
and flight deck*

The largest airships were "rigids," made of stretched cloth over a framework of light metal or wood. Hydrogen-filled gas bags inside the airship gave the lifting force. More than 150 rigids were built between 1900 and 1938. Up to 650 ft (200 m) long and powered by internal combustion engines, they carried passengers on long-distance flights. Some were used to bomb cities during World War I. Hydrogen burns easily, and many rigids were lost in fires.

1915•
ALL-METAL MONOPLANE *Germany*

At a time when most aircraft were still mainly built of wood, Hugo Junkers in Germany designed his all-metal J1 monoplane. Its revolutionary steel wings were fully cantilevered – that is, built straight out from the body of the aircraft, with no extra wires or struts to support them. With its streamlined exterior, the J1 achieved a speed of 105 mph (170 kph) and was the first of a line of successful Junkers aircraft.

*Sober gray paintwork
contributed to the
motorcycle's name.*

Headlight

•1917
RECONNAISSANCE FIGHTER *Germany*

With the outbreak of World War I in 1914, thousands of new aircraft were produced. Many were reconnaissance fighters, such as the German LVG C.VI. Their role was to observe and photograph enemy activity. They were equipped with machine guns to defend themselves or attack other aircraft.

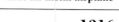

**Junkers J1, 1915 – the world's
first all-metal airplane**

•1916
TANK *UK/France*

In World War I, British and French engineers developed armored vehicles that ran on metal caterpillar tracks. These tracks enabled the vehicles to cross rough ground by laying down their own metal "road" and picking it up behind them. To hide its real purpose from the enemy, the British referred to their vehicle as a water tank, and the name has stuck.

K type bus, 1919–32

1919•
MOTOR BUS *England*

By placing the driver alongside the engine instead of behind it, the designers of the AEC K type double-decker produced a version of the famous red London bus that could seat 46 passengers. Forward-facing seats inside were another innovation, but upstairs passengers were still unprotected from the weather, and the bus ran on solid rubber tires, not pneumatic ones.

Silent Gray Fellow, 1912

*Pedals are used to
start the engine and
set the motorcycle in
motion because it has
no starter or gearbox.*

•1912 HARLEY DAVIDSON *US*

Motorcycles had already evolved into their modern shape when William Harley and the three Davidson brothers began making them in Wisconsin in 1903. Motorcycles were more affordable than cars, and Harley-Davidson machines such as the single cylinder Silent Gray Fellow were soon contributing to a boom in sales. Its top speed was 45 mph (72 kph).

**British tank,
1916**

**Model of the luxury
liner *Mauretania*, 1907**

Lifeboat

*Swiveling
gun turret*

•1915 BATTLESHIP *Germany*

Powerful and heavily armored battleships controlled the oceans during World War I. Earlier warships carried their guns along each side (*see* **WARSHIP 1511**), but battleships now carried their weaponry on deck. The guns were mounted in pairs in swiveling turrets along the ship's centerline, so that its formidable firepower could be pointed in any direction.

**Model of the
German
battleship
Baden, 1915**

US destroyer, 1917

•1917 DESTROYER *US*

A destroyer's role in World War I was to protect other ships, particularly from attack by a new and very destructive weapon – the torpedo. This was an underwater missile, usually launched from a submarine. Destroyers (originally called "torpedo-boat destroyers") were smaller and faster than battleships, and carried their own guns and torpedo-launching equipment.

•**1910** Frenchman Henri Fabre builds a seaplane – an airplane that can take off and land on water.
•**1911** In the US, a white line is used to mark the center of roads.
•**1911** In India, 6,500 letters are carried by airplane – probably the world's first official airmail delivery.
•**1912** The liner *Titanic*, the largest ever launched, hits an iceberg and sinks with the loss of 1,513 lives.
•**1912** In the US, electric starters are now standard in all Cadillac cars. Other cars are still started by turning a crank handle at the front.

•**1912** SOS is now a universal distress signal for ships and aircraft.
•**1913** Travel from Europe to the Far East takes less than two weeks on the Trans-Siberian Railroad.
•**1913** Ford assembles Model Ts on a moving conveyor belt.
•**1913** Grand Central railroad station – the largest in the world – opens in New York.
•**1914** The world's first traffic lights are used in Cleveland, Ohio.
•**1914** The 51-mile (82-km) Panama Canal opens, linking the Atlantic and Pacific Oceans.

The sinking of the *Titanic*, 1912

• **1915** A Hawaiian introduces surfboarding to Australia, where it soon becomes popular.
•**1915** German airships drop bombs on Britain.
•**1915** The German Junkers J1 is the first all-metal airplane.
•**1916** Some American cars are fitted with vacuum-operated windshield wipers. Electric wipers will follow soon in 1923.
•**1917** A railroad is completed across Australia. It has a 300-mile (480-km) stretch without a single bend.

•**1919** The first nonstop flight across the Atlantic is made by British aviators John Alcock and Arthur Whitten-Brown in a Vickers Vimy biplane, a two-winged aircraft. The journey from Newfoundland takes 16.5 hours, and ends safely with a crash-landing in an Irish bog. Two weeks later, the British airship R34 also makes a nonstop crossing.
•**1919** Daily passenger flights are set up between London, England, and Paris, France. This is the first regular international service.

1920   1925

| 1920 | 1921 | | 1924 | 1925 | 1926 | 1927 |

AIR

Rotor blade

Cierva C-30, 1932

K4232

The autogiro's upswept tailplane keeps the fuselage steady. It counter-balances the force created by the rotor blade overhead.

Fuselage of steel tubing covered with fabric

A conventional propeller at the front pulls the aircraft forward for takeoff and normal flight.

1923·
AUTOGIRO *Spain/UK*

An autogiro is a small airplane with no wings. It is pulled forward by a motor-driven propeller at the front. The large overhead rotor is not turned by its own motor – as on a helicopter – but is blown around as the autogiro moves forward. This lifts the autogiro off the ground. The first autogiro was made by Spaniard Juan de la Cierva in 1923.

The flying doctor makes a call

·1926
RACING SEAPLANE *Italy*

Streamlined racing seaplanes, designed to take off and land on water, took part each year in the international Schneider Trophy contest. First place in the 1926 race went to Italy's Macchi M.39, whose 800-hp (600-kW) Fiat engine gave it a top speed of 260 mph (420 kph). The winner of the 1931 Trophy, the Supermarine S6B was the forerunner of Britain's successful Spitfire fighter. *See* FIGHTERS AND BOMBERS 1940–45.

Macchi M.39, 1926 Schneider Trophy winner

·1928
FLYING DOCTOR *Australia*

Two new technologies, the light airplane and the two-way radio, have come together to provide emergency medical care in sparsely populated parts of the world. Since 1928, Australia's Royal Flying Doctor Service has been a lifeline for people living in isolated areas. The first flying doctor, Dr. K. St. Vincent Welch, flew in a small de Havilland DH–50 aircraft. In its first year, the service treated 255 patients.

LAND

Charabanc, 1926

1926·
MOTOR COACH *UK*

People who did not have their own cars could still enjoy the delights of driving on a country outing by coach – a motorized version of the horse-drawn "charabanc" (French for "carriage with benches"). Some motor charabancs wisely incorporated a folding canopy that could quickly be raised to protect the passengers if it started to rain.

Benz diesel truck, 1923

·1923 DIESEL TRUCK *Germany*

Transporting goods by road became easier when the Benz company introduced its first diesel-powered truck, designed in 1923 and made commercially available in 1924. Diesel engines are more powerful, run on cheaper fuel, and get more miles to the gallon than gasoline engines. By the 1930s, a large number of freight vehicles had diesel engines.

·1928
MOTO GUZZI 500S *Italy*

Motorcycles were at their most popular during the 1920s and 1930s when they met the needs of many people who could not afford a car. The Italian Moto Guzzi company was a leading producer of motorcycles in the 1920s. The design of the single-cylinder 500 cc Moto Guzzi was so advanced that it stayed in production for more than 50 years. The S model was one of the more basic versions.

Moto Guzzi 500S, 1928

WATER

Model of *København* training and cargo ship, 1921

·1921
SAILING BARQUE *Denmark*

The last large sailing ships were built in the early part of the 20th century. Many were steel-hulled "barques," which were economical to run because their rigging could be handled by a fairly small crew. The Danish *København* was a five-masted barque used for young sailors. It also carried cargo to subsidize the cost of training.

·1924 OIL TANKER *UK*

As demand for gasoline grew, specialized ships called oil tankers were used to carry crude oil and the products made from it. As with all tankers up until the 1990s, the hull of the 6,600-ton (6,000-tonne) *Wellfield*, shown below, was basically a large floating tank with compartments into which the oil was poured.

Model of the oil tanker *Wellfield*, 1924

The submarine was driven by propellers at the stern.

Tanks in the hull took in water to make the submarine dive, and expelled water to make the submarine rise to the surface.

The crew's quarters and the 600-hp (450-kW) diesel engine were at the stern of the ship.

MILESTONES

1920–1929

- **1920** The British ship *Fullagar* is the first to be built from metal plates that are welded together rather than riveted.
- **1920** The American Dayton-Wright RB racing monoplane is the first with a retractable landing gear.
- **1921** In the US, the Duesenberg Model A is the first car with hydraulic brakes. Pressure on the brake pedal is transmitted to the wheels through tubes filled with liquid.
- **1921** American chemists discover that adding a compound called tetraethyl lead to gasoline reduces "knocking," premature explosions in car engines.

- **1923** The Bronx River Parkway opens in the US – the first ever limited-access highway. Motorists can join or leave it only at specially built interchanges.
- **1923** The German government plans a major road-building program that will complete 2,050 miles (3,300 km) of autobahns by 1939.
- **1923** Britain's *Hermes* and Japan's *Hosho* are the world's first specially built aircraft carriers.
- **1924** The first round-the-world flight is made by two Douglas biplanes. The aircraft travel 27,600 miles (44,000 km) over a period of 5.5 months.

Robert Goddard beside his rocket, 1926

- **1926** The American scientist Robert Goddard launches the first successful liquid-fueled rocket. Its 2.5-second flight reaches a height of 41 ft (12.5 m).
- **1927** British driver Henry Seagrave reaches 204 mph (328 kph) in his *Sunbeam* car.
- **1927** Charles Lindbergh makes the first solo nonstop transatlantic flight in his Ryan monoplane *Spirit of St. Louis*.
- **1927** The US's Fageol Twin Coach sets a new style in bus design, with its flat front and driver-operated doors.
- **1927** Japan's first underground railroad opens in Tokyo.

- **1928** In the UK, Frank Whittle has the idea of using jet propulsion for aircraft, but will not build his first jet engine until 1937.
- **1928** A transcontinental bus service operates across the US. It uses "nite coaches" with sleeping facilities.
- **1929** General Motors introduces the synchromesh gearbox on its Cadillac cars. Synchromesh eventually becomes standard, making gear-changing easier.
- **1929** The airship *Graf Zeppelin* flies around the world in 21 days.
- **1929** Five million new cars are made in the US this year.

1930

1935

Flight deck

Landing gear folds into wing after takeoff.

Boeing 247D, 1933

550-hp (410-kW) air-cooled radial engine

Propeller blades swivel to give the right angle, or pitch, for takeoff, landing, or cruising.

•1933 BOEING 247 *US*

As new airliners were developed, flying began to be an everyday means of transportation for many people, especially in the US. The twin-engined Boeing 247 could whisk its ten passengers over a distance of 600 miles (1,000 km) in only four hours. Its novel features included an all-metal skin and wheels that could be pulled up into the wings to reduce drag when the plane was airborne.

•1935 DOUGLAS DC3 *US*

No airliner has sold in such large numbers as the Douglas DC3, which carried up to 21 passengers at 170 mph (270 kph). By 1939, these dependable aircraft had become the workhorses of the skies, transporting 90 percent of all airline passengers. The DC3, later renamed Skytrain or Dakota, went on to provide vital services during World War II and after.

A Douglas DC3, still in service in 1981

Greyhound bus, 1931

•1931 INTERCITY BUS *US*

Improved roads in the US led to the setting up of many intercity bus routes. By 1931, the Greyhound bus companies had a 40,000-mile (65,000-km) network linking cities and vacation spots in the US, Mexico, and Canada. Since the 1930s, intercity buses have provided comfortable, cheap transportation over long distances.

1934• STREAMLINER TRAIN *US*

Futuristic-looking streamlined trains were introduced on long-distance lines in the US, hauled not by steam locomotives but by diesel-electrics. Streamliners were popular for their speed as well as their comfort, particularly after Union Pacific's air-conditioned M–10001 train crossed the continent from San Francisco to New York in a record time of only 57 hours.

Union Pacific M–10000 City of Salina, 1934

Heinkel 178, 1939

1939• JET AIRCRAFT *Germany*

There is a limit to how fast a propeller-driven airplane can travel, so designers looking for speed turned to another type of engine – the turbojet. The earliest pioneer was German engineer Hans von Ohain, who installed a jet engine in the experimental Heinkel 178. It flew successfully in August 1939, and later achieved the spectacular speed of 470 mph (755 kph).

The high hood conceals a powerful 4.5-liter engine.

Golf-club hatch

Whitewall tires

Side view of Auburn 851 Speedster, 1935

V-shaped radiator grill

•1935 SPORTS CAR *US*

American cars of the 1930s were often large, powerful, and stylish. Like the Auburn 851 Speedster, many of them were designed more to impress than to be practical motor vehicles. The Auburn was 20 ft (6 m) long, but was only a two-seater and had little room for luggage – although it did have a special locker for stowing golf clubs!

Front view of Auburn 851 Speedster, 1935

Model of U-25: launched 1936, sunk 1940

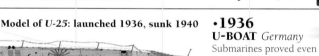

The conning tower gives a good viewing position when the submarine is on the surface.

Fins on each side of the hull swivel to deflect the flow of water, raising or lowering the submarine's nose.

•1930 STEAM TUG *UK*

Tugs are small, powerful boats used to maneuver large ships into and out of dock, and to push or pull long chains of river barges. The large funnel reflects the power of the huge steam or diesel engine that fills much of a tug's hull space. Tugs are also used for fire fighting, and for helping broken down or damaged ships.

Model of a steam tug, c.1930

•1936 U-BOAT *Germany*

Submarines proved even more deadly in World War II than they had in World War I. A fleet of German U-boats – short for "Unterseebooten" (undersea boats) – was developed from prototypes like the one shown here. U-25 carried 14 torpedoes and could remain submerged for long periods. On the move, it had to resurface every 78 miles (125 km) to replenish its air supplies.

1939• BATTLESHIP *Germany*

With eight huge guns, the German battleship *Bismarck* was a threat to Atlantic shipping routes in World War II. Launched in 1939, *Bismarck* was sunk by gunfire and torpedoes from British ships and aircraft in 1941. By the end of the war, aircraft carriers had become more important than battleships in naval warfare.

See AIRCRAFT CARRIER 1946.

Model of *Bismarck*, 1939

•**1930s** Heavy trucks, often with 6 or 8 wheels to carry bigger loads, are a common sight on many roads.
•**1930s** Steam locomotives are beginning to give way to diesels and mainline electric services.
•**1930** The German Society for Space Travel opens a site near Berlin to build and test liquid-fueled rockets.
•**1930** Amy Johnson flies solo from England to Australia in 19 days.
•**1931** The British Supermarine S6B seaplane wins the international Schneider Trophy race, averaging 340.1 mph (547.3 kph).

•**1932** The Sydney Harbour Bridge opens in Australia. It carries a dual railroad track, two footpaths, and a road, all suspended from a steel arch.
•**1932** Amelia Earhart is the first woman to fly across the Atlantic solo.
•**1933** The twin-engined Boeing 247 is the first modern-style airliner.
•**1934** In the US, a streamlined diesel-electric train called the Pioneer Zephyr runs nonstop for 1,015 miles (1,633 km) between Denver and Chicago.

The giant *Hindenburg* airship bursts into flames while docking, 1937

•**1935** The first parking meters are used in Oklahoma City, Oklahoma.
•**1935** The Boeing B-17, or "Flying Fortress," is the first four-engined, all metal, monoplane bomber.
•**1935** The Moscow underground railroad opens.
•**1935** The French liner *Normandie* crosses the Atlantic in a record time of 4 days, 3 hours, and 2 minutes.
•**1935** Scottish scientist Robert Watson-Watt uses radio waves to detect aircraft. Radar will become vital for tracking ships and aircraft, and for navigation.

•**1935** In the US, the Douglas DC3 makes it first flight.
•**1936** In Germany, prototypes are made of the Volkswagen Beetle.
•**1937** The Golden Gate Bridge opens in San Francisco, California. For 30 years it will be the longest suspension bridge in the world.
•**1937** The age of the passenger airship ends when the *Hindenburg* explodes in New Jersey.
•**1938** The Boeing 307 is the first airliner with a pressurized cabin.
•**1939** The German Heinkel 178 is the first jet-propelled aircraft.

1940

1940	1941

1945

1945	1946	1947	1948	1949

Supermarine Spitfire and Messerschmitt Me 109

AIR

•1940–45 FIGHTERS AND BOMBERS

In the midair dogfights of World War II, the performance of a fighter plane's engine was almost as crucial as its weapons or the skill of its pilot. British Spitfire and Hurricane fighters had Rolls-Royce engines, while Germany's Messerschmitts had Daimler-Benz engines powered Germany's Messerschmitts. Bombers, too, needed powerful engines – and more of them – in order to carry huge bomb loads for saturation bombing of cities and other targets. America's Boeing B-17 Flying Fortress bomber had four 1,200-hp (900-kW) Wright Cyclone engines, two on each wing.

Boeing B-17 Flying Fortress

•1945 HELICOPTER US

Modern helicopters follow a design pioneered in 1942 by Igor Sikorsky, a Russian-American. His XR–4 helicopter had a large rotor, like an upturned propeller, that raised the helicopter off the ground. The rotor was tilted to move the helicopter forward or backward. A tail rotor acted like a rudder, and stopped the aircraft from spinning around.

Sikorsky R–4 helicopter, 1945

Pilot's seat

Front landing wheel

Engine housing

•1943 LOCKHEED CONSTELLATION US

First used for military transportation, Lockheed's four-engined Constellation entered service as a commercial airliner after World War II. With a range of 2,000 miles (3,200 km), it carried up to 81 passengers at 340 mph (550 kph). The Constellation played an important part in the growth of air travel in the 1950s.

Lockheed Constellation in service in Brazil, 1949

The fins, designed to look like aircraft tailplanes, were purely decorative.

LAND

1941• BIG BOY US

To haul huge freight trains across the Rocky Mountains, the Union Pacific Railroad built the largest ever steam locomotives. Known as "Big Boys," these 130-ft (40-m) long giants had a top speed of 80 mph (130 kph), making them fast as well as powerful. Clouds of black smoke poured from their chimneys because the exhaust contained large amounts of unburned coal particles.

A Big Boy locomotive in steam, 1940s

•1944 JEEP US

The US Army's General Purpose vehicle (GP or "jeep" for short), was designed for battlefield reconnaissance duties. But it was soon being used as an emergency ambulance, a mobile gun platform, and more. Jeeps were light enough to be carried in a glider and dropped by parachute or delivered to beaches in small landing craft.

A jeep emerges from a landing craft, 1944

Huge chromed bumper

Citroën 2CV, 1949

1949• CITROËN 2CV
France

With its tiny engine and "garden-shed" bodywork, Citroën's 2CV was designed as a first car for people in France's rural areas. Although many of its drivers were farmers more used to traveling by horse and cart, they soon found it remarkably spacious and robust.

WATER

1941• LIBERTY SHIP US

In four years during World War II, more than 2,700 cargo steamers were mass-produced in the US to replace ships being sunk by German, Italian, and Japanese submarines. These "Liberty ships" followed a simple, rugged design, using prefabricated parts and a welded steel hull. One ship was built in the record time of 14 days from start to finish.

Studebaker "Water Weasel" amphibious cargo carrier, 1944

•1944 AMPHIBIOUS VEHICLE US

When the Studebaker company added a boatlike body, two rudders, and flotation tanks to its "Weasel" military vehicle, it produced a version that traveled both in water and on land. The amphibious "Water Weasel" had rubber tracks for moving over difficult surfaces such as snow. Its top speed was 36 mph (58 kph) on land, and 4 mph (6 kph) in water.

Many aircraft used on aircraft carriers have wings that fold up to save space on deck.

Radar aerial to identify and track targets

1946• AIRCRAFT CARRIER UK

HMS *Eagle* served in the British Navy for 26 years. Aircraft carriers have changed the nature of sea warfare because their aircraft can attack targets beyond the range of any warship's guns. During takeoff, the aircraft are propelled forward by a device called a catapult, while arrester wires across the deck slow them as they land.

Cranes lift aircraft out of water if they overshoot flight deck.

Model of HMS *Eagle* (1946–72) as it looked in 1964

Derrick lifts cargo on and off ship

Model of a Liberty ship, 1941

MILESTONES

1940–1949

•**1940** Igor Sikorsky's VS-300 is the world's first practical single rotor helicopter.
•**1940** A four-wheel drive General Purpose car, or "jeep," is designed for the US Army.

B-12 snowmobile, early 1940s

•**1941** "Big Boy" locomotives enter service on America's Union Pacific Railroad.
•**1941** In Canada, the Bombardier company introduces the versatile B-12, one of the most successful snowmobiles ever.
•**1941** The first "Liberty ship" is launched in the US.
•**1942** Germany's Messerschmitt Me 262 jet fighter makes its first flight, followed in 1943 by the British Gloster Meteor jet.
•**1944** Germany launches the first of nearly 3,000 V2 armed rockets at targets in the UK and elsewhere.

Liquid-fueled V2 rocket, 1944

•**1945** An American Boeing B-29 bomber drops the first atomic bomb on the Japanese city of Hiroshima.
•**1946** Motorized scooters called Vespas (Italian for "wasp") appear in Italy.
•**1946** In New Mexico, a rocket is fired to a height of 50 miles (80 km). US rocket engineers also begin experimenting with captured V2 rockets. *See* MILESTONES 1944.
•**1947** As demand for gasoline rises, drilling for undersea oil starts in the Gulf of Mexico.

•**1947** Captain "Chuck" Yeager breaks the sound barrier in the Bell X1 rocket-plane. At an altitude of 42,000 ft (12,800 m), he reaches a speed of 670 mph (1,078 kph) – faster than the speed of sound at that height.
•**1947** Soichiro Honda fits war-surplus engines to ordinary bicycles in Japan. By 1960, his Honda company will be the world's leading producer of motorcycles.
•**1949** A US B-50A bomber flies nonstop around the world, refueling in midair four times in the course of its 94-hour flight.
•**1949** The Citroën 2CV car appears in France. People laugh at its odd appearance, but millions will be sold around the world.

1950

1955

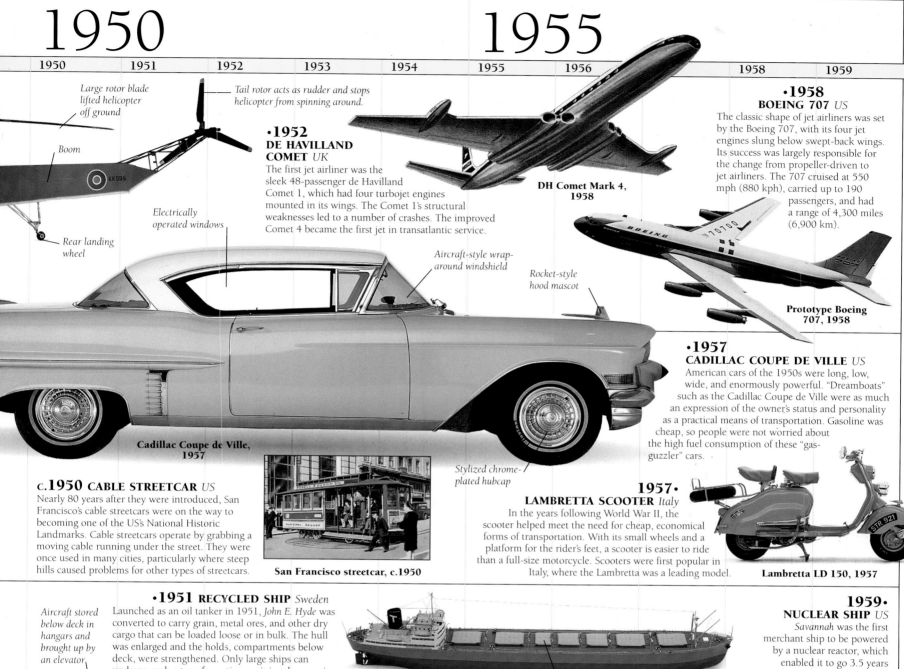

Large rotor blade lifted helicopter off ground

Tail rotor acts as rudder and stops helicopter from spinning around.

Boom

Rear landing wheel

Electrically operated windows

•1952 DE HAVILLAND COMET *UK*
The first jet airliner was the sleek 48-passenger de Havilland Comet 1, which had four turbojet engines mounted in its wings. The Comet 1's structural weaknesses led to a number of crashes. The improved Comet 4 became the first jet in transatlantic service.

DH Comet Mark 4, 1958

Aircraft-style wrap-around windshield

Rocket-style hood mascot

•1958 BOEING 707 *US*
The classic shape of jet airliners was set by the Boeing 707, with its four jet engines slung below swept-back wings. Its success was largely responsible for the change from propeller-driven to jet airliners. The 707 cruised at 550 mph (880 kph), carried up to 190 passengers, and had a range of 4,300 miles (6,900 km).

Prototype Boeing 707, 1958

Cadillac Coupe de Ville, 1957

Stylized chrome-plated hubcap

•1957 CADILLAC COUPE DE VILLE *US*
American cars of the 1950s were long, low, wide, and enormously powerful. "Dreamboats" such as the Cadillac Coupe de Ville were as much an expression of the owner's status and personality as a practical means of transportation. Gasoline was cheap, so people were not worried about the high fuel consumption of these "gas-guzzler" cars.

c.1950 CABLE STREETCAR *US*
Nearly 80 years after they were introduced, San Francisco's cable streetcars were on the way to becoming one of the US's National Historic Landmarks. Cable streetcars operate by grabbing a moving cable running under the street. They were once used in many cities, particularly where steep hills caused problems for other types of streetcars.

San Francisco streetcar, c.1950

1957• LAMBRETTA SCOOTER *Italy*
In the years following World War II, the scooter helped meet the need for cheap, economical forms of transportation. With its small wheels and a platform for the rider's feet, a scooter is easier to ride than a full-size motorcycle. Scooters were first popular in Italy, where the Lambretta was a leading model.

Lambretta LD 150, 1957

Aircraft stored below deck in hangars and brought up by an elevator

•1951 RECYCLED SHIP *Sweden*
Launched as an oil tanker in 1951, *John E. Hyde* was converted to carry grain, metal ores, and other dry cargo that can be loaded loose or in bulk. The hull was enlarged and the holds, compartments below deck, were strengthened. Only large ships can undergo such a transformation, as it involves cutting the ship in halves, both lengthways and widthways, and adding extra sections.

Model of John E. Hyde as dry cargo ship

Separate holds stop cargo from shifting in rough seas.

1959• NUCLEAR SHIP *US*
Savannah was the first merchant ship to be powered by a nuclear reactor, which enabled it to go 3.5 years without refueling. The reactor produced heat by splitting atoms. The heat was then used to generate steam to power turbines. Only a few nuclear-powered merchant ships have been built because they are so expensive to build and operate.

Antiaircraft guns to defend against enemy aircraft

•1955 HOVERCRAFT *UK*
Hovercraft ride on a cushion of high-pressure air that reduces friction between the craft and the surface over which it travels. In 1955, the British engineer Christopher Cockerell made a successful model hovercraft powered by a model airplane engine. The world's first full-sized hovercraft, Cockerell's SR-N1, made its first appearance in 1959.

Cockerell's SR–N1 hovercraft, 1959

Model of NS Savannah, launched 1959

1950–1954

•**1951** The Chrysler Imperial is the first car with power-assisted steering, which uses power from the engine to help turn the steering wheel.
•**1952** The world's first jet airliner, the de Havilland Comet 1, enters service.
•**1953** The Chevrolet Corvette is the first production car to have a plastic body, made from reinforced fiberglass.

Surfing in the 1950s

•**1953** The ancestor of modern surfboards, the polyurethane plastic "Simmons board" (or "Malibu board") goes on sale.
•**1953** The first turboprop airliner, the Vickers Viscount, goes into service. Turboprop engines use a gas turbine to drive a propeller.
•**1954** In the UK, a curious machine nicknamed the "Flying Bedstead" shows that jet aircraft will one day be able to take off vertically by directing their engines' thrust downward.

1955–1959

•**1955** The American submarine *Nautilus* is the first to be powered by a nuclear reactor.
•**1956** The world's first regular hydrofoil service starts between Sicily and mainland Italy.
•**1957** The Soviet Union's *Sputnik 1* is the first artificial satellite to orbit the Earth. A dog called Laika aboard *Sputnik 2* becomes the first living creature in space.
•**1958** Austin's Mini-Minor goes on sale. It will be the UK's best-selling car ever.
•**1958** The Boeing 707, one of the worlds most successful jet airliners, enters service.

•**1959** Seat belts are offered as an optional extra on cars from the Swedish manufacturer Volvo.
•**1959** In the UK, Christopher Cockerell designs the world's first practical hovercraft.
•**1959** The St. Lawrence Seaway opens, allowing ships from the Atlantic to travel 2,400 miles (3,800 km) into the Great Lakes region of North America.
•**1959** The Russian icebreaker *Lenin* is the first non-military ship to have a nuclear reactor.

Laika – the first living creature in space, 1957

1960–2000 A world on the move

SPACE TRAVEL WAS FOR MANY YEARS something that people only read about in books and comics, or saw in science fiction movies. Then, in the 1960s, it suddenly became real. A Russian cosmonaut orbited the Earth in space in 1961; eight years later, American astronauts were walking on the Moon. But manned space flight proved enormously expensive and after 1972, no more journeys to the Moon or planets were planned. Space travelers stayed closer to home, orbiting the Earth in the US's reusable space shuttle or making visits to the Soviet space station *Mir*. Unmanned satellites brought benefits such as better communications between continents, while space probes sent back photographs that greatly increased our knowledge of distant planets. Back on Earth, the use of motor vehicles continued to grow rapidly throughout the world, while the introduction of larger-capacity "jumbo jets" gave a huge boost to air travel.

Vostok rocket

THE SPACE AGE
In 1969, millions of people shared the thrill of humanity's first footsteps on another world, watching live television broadcasts and poring over newspaper reports of the *Apollo 11* mission. It had only been a few short years since the Soviet *Vostok 1* rocket lifted the first person, Yuri Gagarin, into space. Soon there were space stations orbiting the Earth and robot craft landing on Mars. Pictures of the Earth from space reminded people that our planet is itself a sort of spaceship, with a fragile environment.

Apollo 11's "Buzz" Aldrin on the Moon, 1969

The solar panels convert the energy of the Sun's rays into electricity to power the space station's systems and machinery.

Transportation and the consumer society
In the years after 1960, freight transportation of all kinds increased as consumers in richer countries got a taste for goods, such as electrical equipment and cars, that had to be imported from factories thousands of miles away. Similarly, most people in 1900 ate food that had been grown close to where they lived, but by the 1980s, shoppers expected to find exotic foreign fruits and vegetables in their supermarkets all year round. These demands could only be met by more cargo boats and freight aircraft, and heavier semitrailer trucks pounding down the highways at home.

A Soyuz TM spacecraft docks with Mir, carrying a relief crew for the space station.

As many as six spacecraft can dock here at the same time. Cosmonauts enter and leave the space station via an air lock.

Soviet Soyuz TM spacecraft, first launched 1986

THE CHANGING WORLD: 1960 to 2000

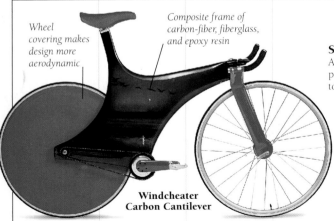

Wheel covering makes design more aerodynamic

Composite frame of carbon-fiber, fiberglass, and epoxy resin

Windcheater Carbon Cantilever

NEW MATERIALS
Sports have made the most of the new high-tech materials. Some of the fastest bicycles have frames made of plastic reinforced with carbon-fiber, which is twice as rigid as steel. Titanium metal is used for wheel bearings because it is as strong as steel but much lighter. Plastic reinforced with fiberglass is used to make race car bodies and hulls for yachts and canoes, while skis and bobsleds are coated with the low-friction plastic PTFE.

SAFETY FIRST
As the number of road deaths increased, public pressure grew for manufacturers to build cars that would give motorists greater protection in an accident. Safety fittings included seat belts and air bags, which inflate instantly to cushion a driver in a crash. Engineers learned to build safer roads, and lawmakers brought in new rules and tougher penalties for bad drivers.

Testing air bags

Swedish X–2000 tilting train, 1990

RAIL REVIVAL
Railroads have fought back against the airplane and the car. New electric services such as the French TGVs and the Japanese Shinkansen routes provide standards of speed and comfort to rival those of airliners. For trains as fast as these, new track without sharp bends often has to be laid. Alternatively, trains can be built with bodies that lean or tilt as they go around bends. These tilting trains can travel safely on normal track at very high speeds.

CIVIL ENGINEERING
Engineering projects provide transportation with its infrastructure – the non-moving parts such as airports, tunnels, highways, and bridges. Most projects involve earth-moving on a vast scale and millions of tons of concrete. Bridges can span gaps of more than 0.6 mile (1 km), while there are rail tunnels more than 30 miles (50 km) long. Huge airstrips can be built by filling shallow areas of sea with rock and rubble to create new land.

Building the Channel Tunnel between England and France

More people, more cars – more problems

For many people, traveling by car became essential to their way of life. But by the 1980s, more people were becoming aware that a price had to be paid for the convenience of owning a car and the freedom to travel. More traffic meant more noise, fumes, and congestion, and more countryside disappearing under concrete as new highways were built. It has been predicted that by the year 2025 there could be more than twice as many vehicles on the world's roads. How will the Earth's atmosphere react to the pollution created by so many cars? And will the world's oil supplies be able to support such a huge volume of traffic? It seems clear that car drivers the world over will have to change their habits in the 21st century.

Rotating television camera

Satellite dish

The *Viking 1* Mars lander, 1976

A never-ending journey?

Whatever happens on Earth, out in space one thing is certain: the longest journey ever undertaken will go steadily on as the space probe *Voyager 2* speeds farther and farther into the icy darkness of the Universe. *Voyager 2* left Earth in 1977 and flew past the planets Jupiter, Saturn, Uranus, and Neptune, before leaving the Solar System forever. This robot explorer will continue its extraordinary voyage of discovery into deep space for many millions of years to come.

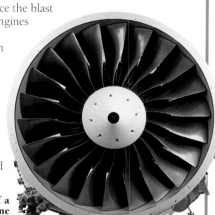

Mir space station, launched 1986

TRANSPORTATION TECHNOLOGY

ROCKET POWER

The simplest rocket is a balloon, blown up and released without closing the nozzle so that it flies around a room. By shooting out air backward, the balloon propels itself forward. Real rockets work in the same way, except that they blast out white-hot gas instead of air. A rocket motor burns fuel so fast that it gives thousands of times more power than any other motor of a similar size. Fuel needs oxygen to burn, so rockets carry an oxidant that allows the fuel to burn in space, where there is no natural oxygen. The space shuttle uses liquid hydrogen as its main fuel, with liquid oxygen as the oxidant.

Space shuttle *Endeavour* on "Crawler," the world's largest land vehicle

JET PROPULSION

Like a rocket, a jet engine obtains its thrust by blowing out a jet of hot gas. Unlike a rocket, it gets its oxygen by using a fan to draw in air at the front. This air is forced into a combustion chamber, where it is mixed with fuel and burned to produce the blast of hot gas. Most jet engines are turbofans, with a huge propellerlike fan at the front. Powered by the engine itself, the fan draws in air for the combustion chamber and sends some air down the outside of the engine. This "jacket" of air adds to the thrust and cuts down noise.

Front view of a turbofan engine

EXPLORING THE DEEP

While astronauts were venturing into space, other explorers were turning toward the Earth's last frontier – the ocean depths. They used diving vessels with strengthened hulls to withstand the huge pressures of the deep ocean. In 1960, Jacques Piccard and Donald Walsh reached a record depth of 7 miles (11 km) in their bathyscaphe *Trieste*. Deep-sea expeditions have also searched for mineral and oil deposits, mapped the seafloor, and found new species of fish and other kinds of life.

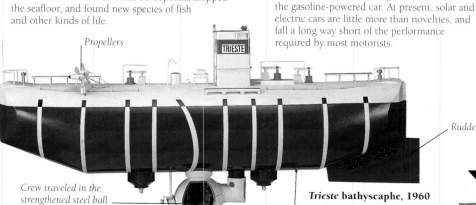

Solar-powered car

Propellers

TRIESTE

ENERGY CRISIS

By 1990, there were 400 million cars in the world. Oil supplies are dwindling, and pollution from car exhausts is damaging the atmosphere. Scientists are still searching for an alternative to the gasoline-powered car. At present, solar and electric cars are little more than novelties, and fall a long way short of the performance required by most motorists.

NEW SHIPS, NEW USES

New types of ships have been built to cope with changing demand. Roll-on roll-off car ferries, with doors at both ends, were developed because people wanted to take their cars with them on vacation. In coastal waters, hovercraft and hydrofoils now provide passengers with high-speed services. Supertankers have replaced luxury liners as the new giants of the seas, carrying oil to meet the world's fuel needs.

Rudder

Hydrofoil, 1980

Crew traveled in the strengthened steel ball

Trieste bathyscaphe, 1960

Washington National Airport, Washington DC

MASS AIR TRAVEL

When wide-bodied jets came into service in the 1970s, air travel became affordable for millions more people. Since then, airports have expanded rapidly to cope with the increasing flood of passengers, but they are often overwhelmed at busy periods. Like miniature towns, major airports now contain shops, restaurants, and even places of worship, with hotels located nearby.

1960

| 1960 | 1961 | | 1964 |

AIR & SPACE

1961 • HAWKER SIDDELEY P.1127 *UK*

The P.1127 first flew in 1961. It could take off vertically and hover, and yet fly much faster than a helicopter. The Harrier jet fighter, developed from the P.1127, entered service in 1969. The swiveling joints on its jet exhausts allow thrust to be directed horizontally for high-speed flight, and downward for takeoff and landing. It does not need a runway and can stop and turn in mid-flight.

Sloping wings

Front view of Hawker Harrier GR5, 1989

Disposable fuel pod

Air intake

Swiveling nozzle on exhaust of jet engine

Vostok 1, 1961

• 1961 *VOSTOK 1 USSR*

The USSR startled the world on April 12, 1961, when cosmonaut Yuri Gagarin became the first person in space. In his *Vostok 1* spacecraft, he made a single orbit of the Earth on a journey lasting 108 minutes. On his return to Earth, Gagarin ejected from the spacecraft at a height of 23,000 ft (7,000 m) and landed safely by parachute.

F-111 with wings forward

• 1964 GENERAL DYNAMICS F-111 *US*

It is difficult to design aircraft that can fly at high supersonic speeds but also perform well at lower, subsonic speeds. General Dynamics's F-111, first flown in 1964, overcame this problem with "swing-wings." At low speeds, the wings are swung forward, as on normal aircraft. For supersonic flight, the wings are folded back, giving a smaller wing area and a more aerodynamic "delta" shape.

F-111 with wings partially swept back

LAND

The large sail, like that of a modern sailboard, can be moved from side to side to catch the wind.

The Mini's great cornering ability was the result of its low center of gravity and wheel placement at the extreme corners of the car.

Spotlight for night rallying

NSU Spyder, 1964

24PK

Steering oar

Austin Mini-Cooper S, 1963

• 1963 NSU SPYDER *Germany*

Germany's NSU Spyder was the first car to have a new type of engine called a Wankel engine. This small, lightweight, yet powerful engine used a triangular piston rotating in an oval chamber.

• 1963 AUSTIN MINI-COOPER *UK*

The Austin Mini-Cooper was a high-performance version of the UK's Mini-Minor, which was first produced in 1958. The Mini was the first front-wheel-drive car to have its engine and gearbox mounted transversely, or parallel to the axle. Most cars today have this layout.

• 1964 BULLET TRAIN *Japan*

Japan's electric Shinkansen, or "new high-speed railroad," opened between Tokyo and Osaka in 1964. Its 12-car "bullet trains" were the world's fastest, capable of 130 mph (210 kph). The passengers enjoyed smooth traveling, good sound insulation, and comfortable, open-plan cars with aircraft-style seats. *See* TGV 1981.

Bullet train passing Mt. Fuji

WATER

The "daggerboard" is pushed down at sea to stop the raft from drifting sideways.

France, 1962

Jangada, 1960

The tapered raft is made of logs lashed or pinned together.

c.1960 JANGADA *Brazil*

Long before windsurfing became a leisure craze, Brazilian aces were skimming across the sea on jangadas. These traditional rafts are still used for fishing up to 30 miles (50 km) off the east coast of Brazil. Similar craft have been used in South America for at least 400 years. *See* SAILBOARD 1977.

Roller for moving raft down beach into sea

Fishermen strap themselves to the deck when they sleep, so they are not washed overboard.

• 1962 *FRANCE France*

At 1,035 ft (301 m), the 73,000-ton (66,000-tonne) *France* was the world's longest ship. It was designed to carry 2,000 passengers or more between Europe and America. But the luxury transatlantic liners gradually lost more and more customers to jet airliners. *France* was renamed *Norway*, and started a new life as a cruise ship.

• 1963 LIGHTSHIP *UK*

Lightships are unpowered vessels that are towed out to sea and moored over offshore obstructions such as sandbanks. A diesel generator provides electricity for the warning light and supplies the crew's needs. Some modern lightships are automatic, controlled by radio signals from the shore.

Model of Kentish Knock lightship, 1963

KENTISH KNOCK

MILESTONES

1960–1964

• **1960** The world's airlines now carry 100 million passengers a year.
• **1960** *Triton*, the US Navy's nuclear submarine, goes around the world in 85 days, without surfacing.
• **1961** The Hawker P.1127 "jump-jet" makes its first successful vertical takeoff and landing.
• **1961** Cosmonaut Yuri Gagarin from the USSR becomes the first person in space in *Vostok 1*.
• **1961** Alan B. Shepard becomes the first American in space when he makes a 15-minute sub-orbital flight.

Skateboard enthusiasts in Rome, Italy, early 1960s

• **1961** US President John F. Kennedy announces that his country will send astronauts to the Moon before 1970.
• **1962** John H. Glenn becomes the first American in orbit aboard *Friendship 7*.
• **1962** In England, Alex Moulton patents a new bicycle design with much smaller wheels than normal bicycles.
• **1963** Improvements in the design of boards mean that more people are taking up skateboarding.
• **1963** Germany's NSU Spyder is the first car to have a Wankel engine.
• **1963** Valentina Tereshkova of the USSR is the first woman in space.

Valentina Tereshkova, first woman in space, 1963

• **1964** "Bullet trains" – the world's fastest – enter service in Japan.
• **1964** Jerrie Mock of the US becomes the first woman to fly solo around the world.
• **1964** Englishman Donald Campbell pushes the world land speed record up to 403 mph (648 kph) in his car *Bluebird II*, and drives a speedboat at 276 mph (445 kph).
• **1964** Three Soviet astronauts orbit the Earth 17 times in *Voskhod 1*.
• **1964** America's Lockheed SR-71A Blackbird flies at three times the speed of sound. *See* MILESTONES 1976.

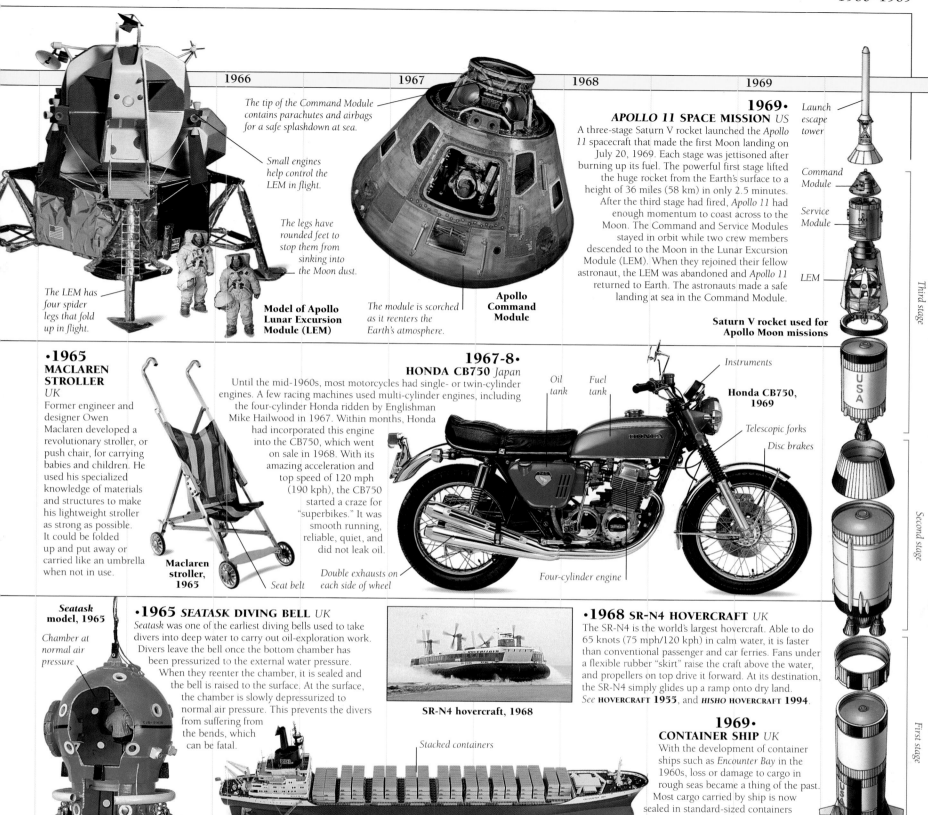

1966 | **1967** | **1968** | **1969**

The tip of the Command Module contains parachutes and airbags for a safe splashdown at sea.

Small engines help control the LEM in flight.

The legs have rounded feet to stop them from sinking into the Moon dust.

The LEM has four spider legs that fold up in flight.

Model of Apollo Lunar Excursion Module (LEM)

The module is scorched as it reenters the Earth's atmosphere.

Apollo Command Module

1969•
APOLLO 11 SPACE MISSION US

A three-stage Saturn V rocket launched the *Apollo 11* spacecraft that made the first Moon landing on July 20, 1969. Each stage was jettisoned after burning up its fuel. The powerful first stage lifted the huge rocket from the Earth's surface to a height of 36 miles (58 km) in only 2.5 minutes. After the third stage had fired, *Apollo 11* had enough momentum to coast across to the Moon. The Command and Service Modules stayed in orbit while two crew members descended to the Moon in the Lunar Excursion Module (LEM). When they rejoined their fellow astronaut, the LEM was abandoned and *Apollo 11* returned to Earth. The astronauts made a safe landing at sea in the Command Module.

Launch escape tower

Command Module

Service Module

LEM

Third stage

Saturn V rocket used for Apollo Moon missions

•1965
MACLAREN STROLLER
UK

Former engineer and designer Owen Maclaren developed a revolutionary stroller, or push chair, for carrying babies and children. He used his specialized knowledge of materials and structures to make his lightweight stroller as strong as possible. It could be folded up and put away or carried like an umbrella when not in use.

Maclaren stroller, 1965

Seat belt

1967-8•
HONDA CB750 *Japan*

Until the mid-1960s, most motorcycles had single- or twin-cylinder engines. A few racing machines used multi-cylinder engines, including the four-cylinder Honda ridden by Englishman Mike Hailwood in 1967. Within months, Honda had incorporated this engine into the CB750, which went on sale in 1968. With its amazing acceleration and top speed of 120 mph (190 kph), the CB750 started a craze for "superbikes." It was smooth running, reliable, quiet, and did not leak oil.

Oil tank | *Fuel tank* | *Instruments*

Honda CB750, 1969

Telescopic forks

Disc brakes

Double exhausts on each side of wheel

Four-cylinder engine

Second stage

•1965 SEATASK DIVING BELL *UK*

Seatask was one of the earliest diving bells used to take divers into deep water to carry out oil-exploration work. Divers leave the bell once the bottom chamber has been pressurized to the external water pressure. When they reenter the chamber, it is sealed and the bell is raised to the surface. At the surface, the chamber is slowly depressurized to normal air pressure. This prevents the divers from suffering from the bends, which can be fatal.

Seatask model, 1965

Chamber at normal air pressure

Decompression chamber

Entry hatch

SR-N4 hovercraft, 1968

•1968 SR-N4 HOVERCRAFT *UK*

The SR-N4 is the world's largest hovercraft. Able to do 65 knots (75 mph/120 km) in calm water, it is faster than conventional passenger and car ferries. Fans under a flexible rubber "skirt" raise the craft above the water, and propellers on top drive it forward. At its destination, the SR-N4 simply glides up a ramp onto dry land.
See **HOVERCRAFT 1955**, *and* **HISHO HOVERCRAFT 1994**.

1969•
CONTAINER SHIP *UK*

With the development of container ships such as *Encounter Bay* in the 1960s, loss or damage to cargo in rough seas became a thing of the past. Most cargo carried by ship is now sealed in standard-sized containers that are secured by guide rails and racks on the ship. On land, the containers fit onto specially built trucks or railroad cars.

Stacked containers

Model of *Encounter Bay* container ship, 1969

First stage

1965–1969

• **1965** Much sea cargo is now carried in standard pre-packed containers aboard specially designed container ships.

• **1965** In the US, Craig Breedlove sets a land speed record of 601 mph (967 kph) in his jet-propelled car *Spirit of America*.

• **1965** At London's Heathrow airport, a Hawker Siddeley Trident airliner makes the first automated landing by a scheduled airline flight.

• **1966** Controversy over an American book titled *Unsafe at Any Speed* makes car manufacturers in the US and elsewhere conscious of the need to build safer cars.

First automated landing, by scheduled airline flight, 1965

• **1967** In the US, the rocket-powered X-15A-2 research aircraft reaches a speed of 4,535 mph (7,300 kph).

• **1967** The Transit navigation system is in commercial use. It allows land, sea, and air travelers to find their location by receiving radio waves from satellites.

• **1967** The first Saturn V rocket – the type that will eventually take people to the Moon – makes a successful test flight.

• **1968** The US introduces new laws to reduce vehicle exhaust fumes.

• **1968** The Soviet Tupolev Tu-144 is the first supersonic airliner to fly. It never goes into full service, and will crash at the Paris Air show in 1973.

• **1968** The SR-N4 hovercraft enters service between England and France.

• **1969** American astronauts Eugene Cernan, John Young, and Thomas Stafford become the fastest humans ever when their *Apollo 10* spacecraft reaches 24,791 mph (39,897 kph).

• **1969** The US's *Apollo 11* astronauts, Neil Armstrong and Buzz Aldrin, become the first people to visit another world when they land on the Moon.

• **1969** The Anglo-French supersonic airliner Concorde flies for the first time. It begins a seven-year program of rigorous testing. *See* **CONCORDE 1976**.

• **1969** The Boeing 747 makes its first flight. *See* **BOEING 747 1970**.

1970

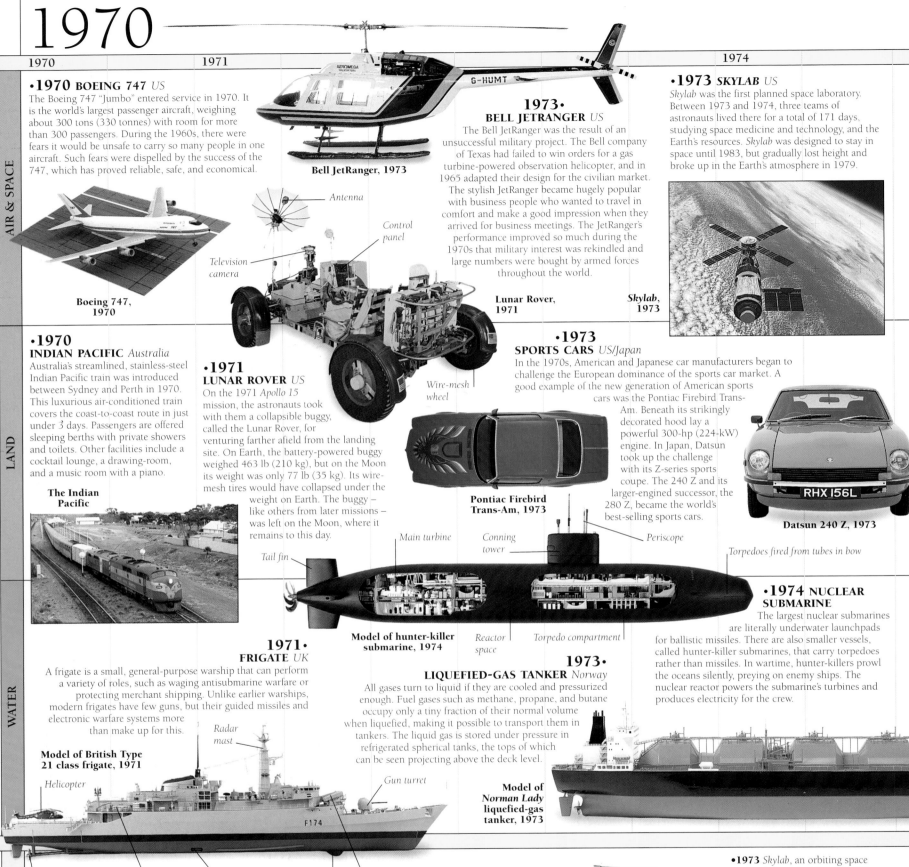

AIR & SPACE

•1970 BOEING 747 US
The Boeing 747 "Jumbo" entered service in 1970. It is the world's largest passenger aircraft, weighing about 300 tons (330 tonnes) with room for more than 300 passengers. During the 1960s, there were fears it would be unsafe to carry so many people in one aircraft. Such fears were dispelled by the success of the 747, which has proved reliable, safe, and economical.

Boeing 747, 1970

1973•
BELL JETRANGER US
The Bell JetRanger was the result of an unsuccessful military project. The Bell company of Texas had failed to win orders for a gas turbine-powered observation helicopter, and in 1965 adapted their design for the civilian market. The stylish JetRanger became hugely popular with business people who wanted to travel in comfort and make a good impression when they arrived for business meetings. The JetRanger's performance improved so much during the 1970s that military interest was rekindled and large numbers were bought by armed forces throughout the world.

Bell JetRanger, 1973

Antenna

Control panel

Television camera

Lunar Rover, 1971

Skylab, 1973

•1973 SKYLAB US
Skylab was the first planned space laboratory. Between 1973 and 1974, three teams of astronauts lived there for a total of 171 days, studying space medicine and technology, and the Earth's resources. *Skylab* was designed to stay in space until 1983, but gradually lost height and broke up in the Earth's atmosphere in 1979.

LAND

•1970 INDIAN PACIFIC Australia
Australia's streamlined, stainless-steel Indian Pacific train was introduced between Sydney and Perth in 1970. This luxurious air-conditioned train covers the coast-to-coast route in just under 3 days. Passengers are offered sleeping berths with private showers and toilets. Other facilities include a cocktail lounge, a drawing-room, and a music room with a piano.

The Indian Pacific

•1971 LUNAR ROVER US
On the 1971 *Apollo 15* mission, the astronauts took with them a collapsible buggy, called the Lunar Rover, for venturing farther afield from the landing site. On Earth, the battery-powered buggy weighed 463 lb (210 kg), but on the Moon its weight was only 77 lb (35 kg). Its wire-mesh tires would have collapsed under the weight on Earth. The buggy – like others from later missions – was left on the Moon, where it remains to this day.

Wire-mesh wheel

•1973 SPORTS CARS US/Japan
In the 1970s, American and Japanese car manufacturers began to challenge the European dominance of the sports car market. A good example of the new generation of American sports cars was the Pontiac Firebird Trans-Am. Beneath its strikingly decorated hood lay a powerful 300-hp (224-kW) engine. In Japan, Datsun took up the challenge with its Z-series sports coupe. The 240 Z and its larger-engined successor, the 280 Z, became the world's best-selling sports cars.

Pontiac Firebird Trans-Am, 1973

Datsun 240 Z, 1973

RHX 156L

Tail fin

Main turbine

Conning tower

Periscope

Torpedoes fired from tubes in bow

WATER

•1971 FRIGATE UK
A frigate is a small, general-purpose warship that can perform a variety of roles, such as waging antisubmarine warfare or protecting merchant shipping. Unlike earlier warships, modern frigates have few guns, but their guided missiles and electronic warfare systems more than make up for this.

Model of British Type 21 class frigate, 1971

Radar mast

Helicopter

Model of hunter-killer submarine, 1974

Reactor space

Torpedo compartment

1973•
LIQUEFIED-GAS TANKER Norway
All gases turn to liquid if they are cooled and pressurized enough. Fuel gases such as methane, propane, and butane occupy only a tiny fraction of their normal volume when liquefied, making it possible to transport them in tankers. The liquid gas is stored under pressure in refrigerated spherical tanks, the tops of which can be seen projecting above the deck level.

Gun turret

Model of Norman Lady liquefied-gas tanker, 1973

•1974 NUCLEAR SUBMARINE
The largest nuclear submarines are literally underwater launchpads for ballistic missiles. There are also smaller vessels, called hunter-killer submarines, that carry torpedoes rather than missiles. In wartime, hunter-killers prowl the oceans silently, preying on enemy ships. The nuclear reactor powers the submarine's turbines and produces electricity for the crew.

F174

Variable pitch propeller   *Torpedo tube*   *Stabilizer*   *Sonar bulge*   *Missile launcher*

MILESTONES

•**1970s** Hydrofoils (boats with hulls that lift out of the water on "wings") are becoming more common on rivers and lakes, particularly in the Soviet Union.
•**1970** The new 2,460-mile (3,960-km) Trans-Australia Railroad opens, linking Sydney and Perth.
•**1970** Two Sikorsky HH-53C helicopters are the first to fly across the Pacific nonstop, refueling in flight.

•**1970** An explosion in *Apollo 13* puts the lives of three American astronauts at risk on their way to the Moon. By improvization, they survive for four days, returning safely to Earth.
•**1970** Three Soviet cosmonauts spend 24 days in *Salyut 1*, the first space station to orbit the Earth. All three die as they prepare to return to Earth because of a malfunction aboard their spacecraft.

•**1971** American astronauts tour the Moon in a lightweight electric car called the Lunar Rover.
•**1972** Astronauts say good-bye to the Moon at the end of the *Apollo 17* mission. No one else will visit the Earth's satellite in the 20th century.
•**1973** Gasoline costs soar as Middle Eastern countries raise oil prices. As a result, smaller, more efficient cars start to become more popular.

Lining up during the gas crisis of 1973

•**1973** *Skylab*, an orbiting space station, is launched from the US.
•**1973** A suspension bridge opens across the Bosporus at Istanbul, Turkey, linking Europe and Asia.
•**1974** Only 45,000 people die in road accidents in the US this year, compared with 54,000 in 1973. The fall is partly the result of a new 55 mph (88 kph) speed limit.
•**1974** Oil is now transported around the world in huge ships called supertankers.

1975

Hang glider c.1975

•1975 HANG GLIDER

Hang gliding was well established by the mid-1970s. A hang glider is really just a huge wing with a harness and framework below to hold the pilot. To launch the glider, the pilot simply runs downhill into the wind. Like a normal glider, a hang glider soars on currents of rising air. The pilot shifts his or her body to control the flight. A hang glider can be dismantled easily and carried on a car roof. *See* GLIDER 1895.

•1976 CONCORDE *UK/France*

Developed by the British Aircraft Corporation and Aérospatiale of France, the Concorde entered service in 1976. This supersonic airliner can cross the Atlantic Ocean in as little as 3 hours with a cruising speed of 1,453 mph (2,338 kph). The "droop nose" is lowered during takeoff and landing to give a better view out of the cockpit. Its noisy turbojet engines burn twice as much fuel as the quieter turbofans of ordinary airliners. Aircraft moving at supersonic speeds create shock waves that are heard on the ground as a loud boom. For this reason, the Concorde has to travel at subsonic speeds over inhabited areas.

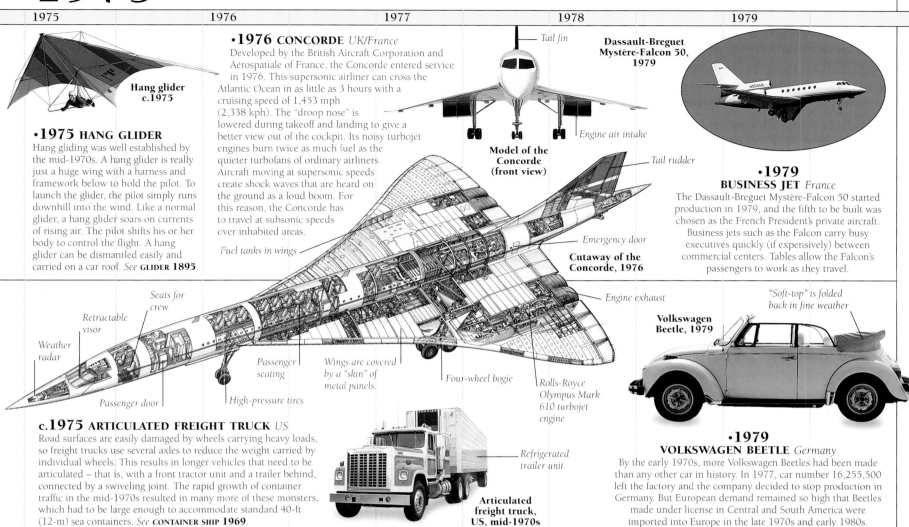

Tail fin

Model of the Concorde (front view)

Engine air intake

Dassault-Breguet Mystère-Falcon 50, 1979

•1979 BUSINESS JET *France*

The Dassault-Breguet Mystère-Falcon 50 started production in 1979, and the fifth to be built was chosen as the French President's private aircraft. Business jets such as the Falcon carry busy executives quickly (if expensively) between commercial centers. Tables allow the Falcon's passengers to work as they travel.

Fuel tanks in wings

Cutaway of the Concorde, 1976

Tail rudder

Emergency door

Seats for crew

Retractable visor

Weather radar

Passenger seating

Wings are covered by a "skin" of metal panels.

Four-wheel bogie

Rolls-Royce Olympus Mark 610 turbojet engine

Engine exhaust

Passenger door

High-pressure tires

"Soft-top" is folded back in fine weather

Volkswagen Beetle, 1979

c.1975 ARTICULATED FREIGHT TRUCK *US*

Road surfaces are easily damaged by wheels carrying heavy loads, so freight trucks use several axles to reduce the weight carried by individual wheels. This results in longer vehicles that need to be articulated – that is, with a front tractor unit and a trailer behind, connected by a swiveling joint. The rapid growth of container traffic in the mid-1970s resulted in many more of these monsters, which had to be large enough to accommodate standard 40-ft (12-m) sea containers. *See* CONTAINER SHIP 1969.

Refrigerated trailer unit

Articulated freight truck, US, mid-1970s

•1979 VOLKSWAGEN BEETLE *Germany*

By the early 1970s, more Volkswagen Beetles had been made than any other car in history. In 1977, car number 16,255,500 left the factory and the company decided to stop production in Germany. But European demand remained so high that Beetles made under license in Central and South America were imported into Europe in the late 1970s and early 1980s.

1975• BOEING JETFOIL *US*

A jetfoil is a hydrofoil driven by a jet of water pumped out of the back. Underwater "wings" on long struts project from the base of the hull. As speed increases, the wings produce lift, and the hull rises clear of the water. This eliminates the drag of water past the hull, allowing speeds of 43 knots (50 mph/80 kph).

A jetfoil rides the waves on its underwater wings

•1977 SAILBOARD *US*

Californian Hoyle Schweitzer took out the first patent on a sailboard in 1968, but controversy surrounds the date of the earliest sailboard, with one claim dating back to 1958. A sailboard is basically a surfboard with a movable triangular sail. Windsurfing grew rapidly as a sport in the late 1970s and early 1980s, with competitions such as wave jumping and distance racing. In 1984, it became part of the Olympic Games.

Sailboard, 1977

•1978 SUPERTANKER

Much of the world's oil is carried in Ultra-Large Crude Carriers (ULCCs), or supertankers. Weighing nearly 550,000 tons (500,000 tonnes), they are 1,475 ft (450 m) long and dwarf all other ships on the sea. They are so big that they take several miles to turn or stop. When fully laden, they sit very low in the water, with waves crashing over the deck – but they are really very stable. Oil is lighter than water, and this makes the ships very buoyant.

Supertanker, 1978

•**1975** Commercial airliners now use inertial navigation, a system that uses an onboard computer to work out the exact position of an aircraft at all times, without reference to anything outside the aircraft.

•**1975** Hijackings and terrorist attacks mean that airports and airlines have to tighten their security operations.

•**1975** The world's first regular jetfoil service starts in Hong Kong.

•**1975** A new law in the US aims to save gasoline by requiring all new cars to get at least 27.5 miles to the gallon (11.7 km to the liter) by 1985.

•**1976** Simultaneous takeoffs by Concorde aircraft in England and France inaugurate the first supersonic passenger services.

•**1976** A world air speed record of 2,193 mph (3,530 kph) is set by a Lockheed SR-71A Blackbird over California.

•**1976** A 1,155-mile (1,859-km) railroad opens between Tanzania and Zambia in Africa.

•**1976** Two American Viking space probes land on Mars. They search for signs of life on the planet, but do not find any.

Robot car manufacturing like this began in the 1970s

•**1977** Computer-controlled robots are now used to make cars, particularly in Japan where 7,000 such robots are at work.

•**1978** Australian Kenneth Warby achieves a world water speed record of 278 knots (320 mph/514 kph) in his boat *Spirit of Australia*.

•**1978** In Utah, *Lightning Bolt*, a twin-engined motorcycle, achieves a motorcycle speed record of 319 mph (513 kph).

•**1978** A solar-powered car runs at 8 mph (13 kph) in England.

•**1979** A model maglev (magnetic levitation) train is tested to a speed of 320 mph (515 kph) in Japan. Maglev trains do not touch their rails, but float just above them by means of strong magnetic forces.

•**1979** A pedal-powered aircraft, *Gossamer Albatross*, is flown from England to France by American racing cyclist Bryan Allen.

1980

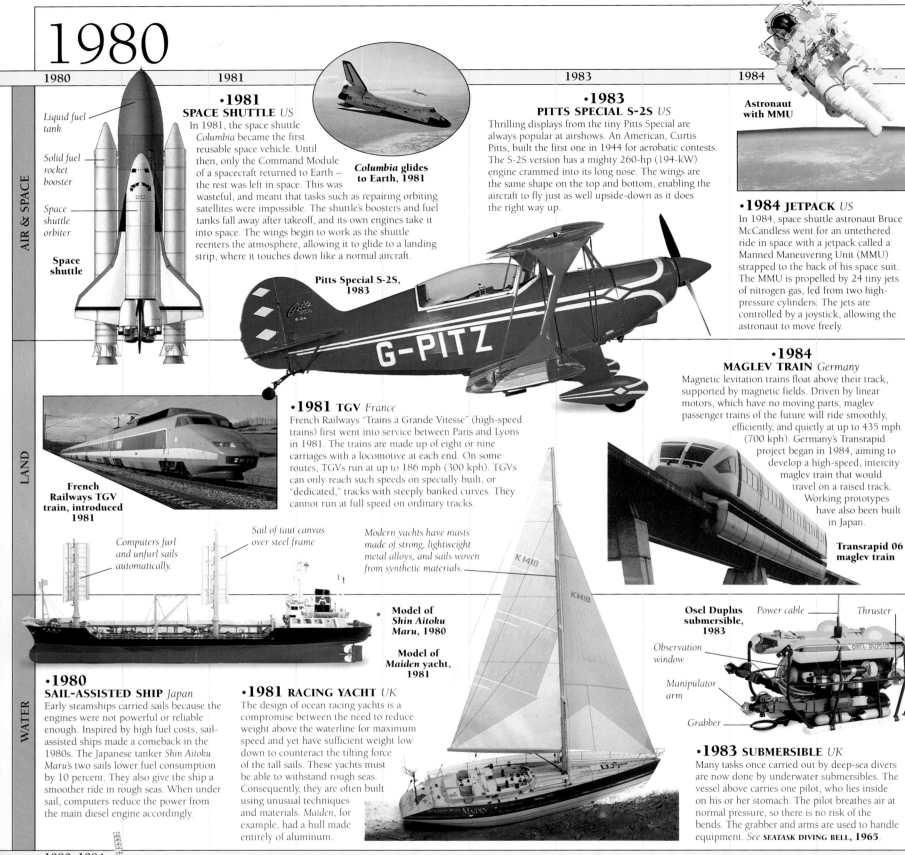

AIR & SPACE

Liquid fuel tank

Solid fuel rocket booster

Space shuttle orbiter

Space shuttle

•1981
SPACE SHUTTLE US
In 1981, the space shuttle *Columbia* became the first reusable space vehicle. Until then, only the Command Module of a spacecraft returned to Earth – the rest was left in space. This was wasteful, and meant that tasks such as repairing orbiting satellites were impossible. The shuttle's boosters and fuel tanks fall away after takeoff, and its own engines take it into space. The wings begin to work as the shuttle reenters the atmosphere, allowing it to glide to a landing strip, where it touches down like a normal aircraft.

Columbia glides to Earth, 1981

•1983
PITTS SPECIAL S-2S US
Thrilling displays from the tiny Pitts Special are always popular at airshows. An American, Curtis Pitts, built the first one in 1944 for aerobatic contests. The S-2S version has a mighty 260-hp (194-kW) engine crammed into its long nose. The wings are the same shape on the top and bottom, enabling the aircraft to fly just as well upside-down as it does the right way up.

Astronaut with MMU

•1984 JETPACK US
In 1984, space shuttle astronaut Bruce McCandless went for an untethered ride in space with a jetpack called a Manned Maneuvering Unit (MMU) strapped to the back of his space suit. The MMU is propelled by 24 tiny jets of nitrogen gas, fed from two high-pressure cylinders. The jets are controlled by a joystick, allowing the astronaut to move freely.

Pitts Special S-2S, 1983

G-PITZ

LAND

•1981 TGV France
French Railways "Trains à Grande Vitesse" (high-speed trains) first went into service between Paris and Lyons in 1981. The trains are made up of eight or nine carriages with a locomotive at each end. On some routes, TGVs run at up to 186 mph (300 kph). TGVs can only reach such speeds on specially built, or "dedicated," tracks with steeply banked curves. They cannot run at full speed on ordinary tracks.

French Railways TGV train, introduced 1981

•1984
MAGLEV TRAIN Germany
Magnetic levitation trains float above their track, supported by magnetic fields. Driven by linear motors, which have no moving parts, maglev passenger trains of the future will ride smoothly, efficiently, and quietly at up to 435 mph (700 kph). Germany's Transrapid project began in 1984, aiming to develop a high-speed, intercity maglev train that would travel on a raised track. Working prototypes have also been built in Japan.

Transrapid 06 maglev train

WATER

Computers furl and unfurl sails automatically.

Sail of taut canvas over steel frame

Modern yachts have masts made of strong, lightweight metal alloys, and sails woven from synthetic materials.

Model of Shin Aitoku Maru, 1980

Model of Maiden yacht, 1981

K 1418

K1418

•1980
SAIL-ASSISTED SHIP Japan
Early steamships carried sails because the engines were not powerful or reliable enough. Inspired by high fuel costs, sail-assisted ships made a comeback in the 1980s. The Japanese tanker *Shin Aitoku Maru*'s two sails lower fuel consumption by 10 percent. They also give the ship a smoother ride in rough seas. When under sail, computers reduce the power from the main diesel engine accordingly.

•1981 RACING YACHT UK
The design of ocean racing yachts is a compromise between the need to reduce weight above the waterline for maximum speed and yet have sufficient weight low down to counteract the tilting force of the tall sails. These yachts must be able to withstand rough seas. Consequently, they are often built using unusual techniques and materials. *Maiden*, for example, had a hull made entirely of aluminum.

Osel Duplus submersible, 1983

Power cable

Thruster

Observation window

Manipulator arm

Grabber

•1983 SUBMERSIBLE UK
Many tasks once carried out by deep-sea divers are now done by underwater submersibles. The vessel above carries one pilot, who lies inside on his or her stomach. The pilot breathes air at normal pressure, so there is no risk of the bends. The grabber and arms are used to handle equipment. See **SEATASK DIVING BELL, 1965**.

MILESTONES

1980–1984

Voyager 2 space probe

Communications antenna

Radioactive power source

•**1980** Seven million motorcycles will be built in the world this year, more than 90 percent of them in Japan.
•**1980** The 10-mile (16-km) long St. Gotthard road tunnel under the Alps opens to traffic.
•**1980** The US Navy's SES-100B hovercraft reaches a record speed of 92 knots (106 mph/170 kph).
•**1981** There are 330 million cars in the world, 80 percent of them in Japan, Europe, and North America. Japan now makes more new cars each year than the US.

•**1981** The space shuttle *Columbia* makes its first successful orbital flight.
•**1981** The American space probe *Voyager 2* passes within 63,000 miles (101,000 km) of Saturn. Launched in 1977, *Voyager 2* has also flown close to Jupiter, and will visit Uranus (1986) and Neptune (1989) before leaving the Solar System forever.
•**1981** A suspension bridge opens over the Humber Estuary in England with a central span of 4,625 ft (1,410 m) – the world's longest.

Humber Bridge, opened 1981

•**1981** In France, the high-speed electric TGV train goes into service.
•**1982** The Japanese Datsun 280 ZX car has an electronic warning voice that speaks to the driver if anything goes wrong.

•**1983** Englishman Richard Noble sets a land speed record of 633 mph (1,019 kph) in the jet-powered *Thrust 2*.
•**1983** Driverless trains run on the new underground railroad in Lille, France.
•**1983** Because of pollution worries, car drivers start to use unleaded fuel.
•**1984** An American astronaut flies freely in space using a jetpack.
•**1984** Three Soviet cosmonauts spend a record 238 days in space in the orbiting station *Salyut 7*.
•**1984** New safety rules in the US insist that all new cars must have air bags and automatic seat belts by 1990.

1985

Northrop B-2 stealth bomber, 1989

Air intake

•1986 RUTAN VOYAGER US

In 1986, the ultra-lightweight *Voyager* made a 25,000-mile (40,000-km) round-the-world flight without refueling. *Voyager* was piloted by Dick Rutan and Jeana Yeager, who took turns at the controls in a cramped cockpit only 24 in (62 cm) wide. *Voyager* was designed by Dick's brother, Burt, with the aim of minimizing its weight and wind resistance, and enabling it to carry as much fuel as possible.

Rutan Voyager, 1986

Illuminated "for hire" sign — *Radio aerial*

•1986 BEECH STARSHIP US

The Beech Aircraft Corporation's 11-seater Starship made headlines for its extensive use of lightweight, plastic-based composite materials. This business aircraft has two "pusher" propellers at the back of the aircraft. The Starship also has wingtip extensions called winglets that improve the wings' performance and save fuel. Like *Voyager*, the Starship was designed by Burt Rutan.

Wing containing fuel tanks

Beech Starship, 1986

•1989 STEALTH BOMBER US

The Northrop B-2, known as the stealth bomber, flew for the first time in 1989. The B-2's role is to make high-speed dashes into enemy territory and deliver a 25-ton (23-tonne) bomb load without being detected. This tailless aircraft, with its jagged shape and concealed engine intakes, is designed to be invisible to enemy radar. Its nonreflective coating and extensive use of nonmetallic composite materials help minimize the reflection of radar signals.

London black cab

c.1985 CITY TAXIS

Taxis – vehicles for hire – are an important form of transportation in cities today. Some taxis have a distinctive look that has become associated with a particular city or part of the world. London's black cabs, for example, have looked virtually the same since 1958. And visitors to New York expect to see yellow taxis. But not all taxis are motor driven. The cycle-rickshaw is a pedal-powered version of earlier ones pulled by people or horses. This energy-efficient "taxi" is typical of many cities in Asia.
See JINRIKISHA 1892.

•1987 MOUNTAIN CABLE CAR New Zealand

In the 19th century, cable cars were used in the Swiss and Austrian Alps to allow visitors to enjoy the fine views. In 1987, new cars were installed on the Austrian-designed system at Bob's Peak in New Zealand. The 4-seater cars hang from a cable 1.5 in (35 mm) thick and travel 1,476 ft (450 m) to the summit. Cars coming down counterbalance those going up, making the system safe and reducing the power needed to pull the cars.

New York yellow taxi

Cable car at Bob's Peak, New Zealand

•1989 MOUNTAIN BIKE Canada

The first all-terrain "mountain bike" was made by Americans Charles Kelly and Gary Fisher in 1981. By the late 1980s, mountain bikes had become popular throughout the world. The robust, lightweight frames, straight handlebars, thick tires, and multiple gears make them ideal both for off-road use and city-center cycling.

Rocky Mountain "Experience," 1989

Chunky tires

Canopy to shelter passengers

Cycle-rickshaw, Bangladesh

Pedals drive a chain that turns the rear axle.

•1986 ICEBREAKER Finland

Icebreakers are vital for keeping seaways open in freezing Arctic waters. Early icebreakers had propellers at the bows as well as at the stern to power through the ice. Instead of bow propellers, Finland's *Otso* icebreaker uses high-pressure air bubbling out of the bow under the waterline. This acts rather like a lubricant, helping the hull slide more easily through the thick mixture of broken ice and cold water.

Otso icebreaker, 1986

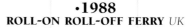

RoRo ferry

•1988 ROLL-ON ROLL-OFF FERRY UK

Roll-on Roll-off (RoRo) car ferries have doors at the bows and the stern so that cars can be driven aboard, parked, and driven off without lengthy maneuvering or handling by cranes. Most of these ships have side and bow thrusters (extra propellers), allowing them to dock in busy ports without using tugs.

•1989 POWERBOAT UK

Offshore powerboat racing became a regular spectacle in the 1980s. Driven by engines similar to those used in race cars, powerboats leap off wave-crests at high speed. The pilots need great skill and quick reflexes to avoid a rough landing that could not only damage the boat, but also cause them serious injury – falling into the sea at high speed can feel like hitting a brick wall.

The hull has a surface layer of stainless steel to protect it in icy water.

Pachanga 27 powerboat, 1989

•**1985** Chicago's O'Hare airport is the world's busiest, with 44,000,000 passengers and 700,000 flights a year.
•**1985** NASA, the American space agency, starts to plan a permanently orbiting space station, but it will only ever be built if the US government agrees to provide massive funding.
•**1986** After a 9-day flight, America's *Voyager* aircraft is the first to fly around the world without refueling.
•**1986** The European *Giotto* space probe flies within 370 miles (600 km) of the nucleus of Halley's Comet.

•**1986** After ten successful flights in the past year, the US space shuttle program is halted when the space shuttle *Challenger* explodes in mid-air, killing all seven crew members.
•**1986** Two Soviet cosmonauts spend 4 months in space, visiting the old *Salyut 7* and the new *Mir* orbiting space stations.
•**1986** Engineers in California consider plans for automatic highways, on which computers will control the spacing of cars and apply brakes when necessary.

•**1988** The new 500-seater Boeing 747-400 Advanced Superjet has a range of 8,000 miles (13,000 km).
•**1988** Work starts on Japan's Akashi suspension bridge. Its 1.2-mile (2-km) central span will be the world's longest.
•**1988** In Japan, the world's longest railroad tunnel is completed. The 33-mile (54-km) Seikan tunnel links the islands of Honshu and Hokkaido.
•**1988** The most powerful diesel engines ever built, capable of 58,000 hp (43 MW), are being installed in new container ships.

A view down the Seikan tunnel in Japan, completed in 1988

•**1988** The Soviet space shuttle orbiter *Buran* makes its only flight.
•**1988** In the US, a solar-powered vehicle called *Sunraycer* reaches a speed of 49 mph (78 kph).
•**1989** The tanker *Exxon Valdez* spills 35,000 tons (32,000 tonnes) of oil after running aground in the Gulf of Alaska. Cleaning up will cost more than 1 billion dollars.
•**1989** The American Northrop B-2 stealth bomber makes its first flight.
•**1989** A 110-ft (33-m) powerboat called *Gentry Eagle* crosses the Atlantic in 2 days and 14 hours.

1990

1990	1991	1992	1993

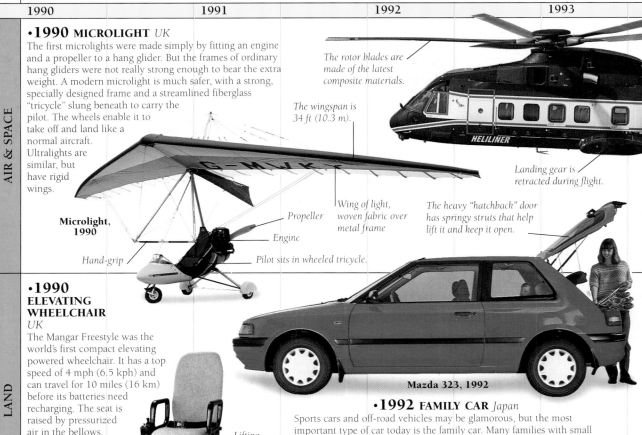

AIR & SPACE

•1990 MICROLIGHT UK

The first microlights were made simply by fitting an engine and a propeller to a hang glider. But the frames of ordinary hang gliders were not really strong enough to bear the extra weight. A modern microlight is much safer, with a strong, specially designed frame and a streamlined fiberglass "tricycle" slung beneath to carry the pilot. The wheels enable it to take off and land like a normal aircraft. Ultralights are similar, but have rigid wings.

The rotor blades are made of the latest composite materials.

The wingspan is 34 ft (10.3 m).

Westland-Agusta EH-101, 1994

Landing gear is retracted during flight.

Microlight, 1990

Propeller

Engine

Hand-grip

Pilot sits in wheeled tricycle.

Wing of light, woven fabric over metal frame

The heavy "hatchback" door has springy struts that help lift it and keep it open.

•1994 WESTLAND-AGUSTA EH-101 UK/Italy

The EH-101 is a multipurpose helicopter that can be used for passenger transportation, air-sea rescue, and military roles. The unusual shape of the rotor blades reduces fuel consumption. In the past, helicopter travel was noisy and unpleasant, but the EH-101 uses ingenious technology to keep vibration, and hence noise, to an absolute minimum. It also minimizes wear and tear on the fuselage.

LAND

•1990 ELEVATING WHEELCHAIR UK

The Mangar Freestyle was the world's first compact elevating powered wheelchair. It has a top speed of 4 mph (6.5 kph) and can travel for 10 miles (16 km) before its batteries need recharging. The seat is raised by pressurized air in the bellows, allowing the user to reach objects far beyond the range of normal wheelchairs.

Mangar Freestyle wheelchair, 1990

Lifting bellows

Electric motor

Mazda 323, 1992

•1992 FAMILY CAR Japan

Sports cars and off-road vehicles may be glamorous, but the most important type of car today is the family car. Many families with small children opt for a three- or five-door hatchback car, such as Japan's Mazda 323. There is room in the back for one or two children, and plenty of storage space. These cars use a transverse engine and front-wheel drive like the original Mini (see **AUSTIN MINI-COOPER 1963**), but they are faster, more comfortable, and more efficient.

•1993 TRIUMPH TROPHY 1200 UK

After 1960, competition from superior Japanese motorcycles caused many European factories to close down. But Europe's surviving manufacturers are now making a comeback. In the early 1990s, these rejuvenated companies launched some up-to-the-minute models, such as the Triumph Trophy 1200, that were among the market's best.

Triumph Trophy 1200, 1993

WATER

•1990 WAVE-PIERCING CATAMARAN Australia

Traditional car and passenger ferries are slowly being replaced by wave-piercing catamarans. These vessels, pioneered by Australia's InCat company, do not ride the waves, they cut right through them. They are faster, and pitch and roll less than ordinary ferries. Powered by water jets, the catamarans have a top speed of 42 knots (48 mph/48 kph).

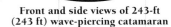

Front and side views of 243-ft (243 ft) wave-piercing catamaran

The MHD boat *Yamoto 1* undergoing trials in 1992

•1992 *YAMOTO 1* Japan

The propulsion system of the revolutionary *Yamoto 1* has no moving parts. Motors and propellers have been eliminated by applying the magneto-hydrodynamic (MHD) principle. When a strong electric current is passed across a tube of water surrounded by powerful magnets, the water is forced through the tube. If the tube is placed beneath the waterline, the flow of water through the tube can be used to propel a boat forward. However, there are fears that passing electric currents through seawater may damage the marine environment.

1994• *HISHO* HOVERCRAFT Japan

Hovercraft development stalled after the 1970s, but now shipbuilders in Japan aim to build huge, fast, cargo-carrying craft by the year 2000. *Hisho*, the forerunner of these craft, was launched in 1994. It can carry 220 tons (200 tonnes) of cargo for 560 miles (900 km) at 54 knots (62 mph/100 kph), in rough seas once impassable to hovercraft.

Hisho, launched 1994

MILESTONES

1990–1994

•**1990** In the US, General Motors shows off its battery-powered Impact car, which can travel 120 miles (190 km) at 55 mph (88 kph) before recharging.
•**1990** A large Australian-built wave-piercing catamaran (twin-hulled boat) crosses the Atlantic in 3 days and 8.5 hours.
•**1990** A French TGV train achieves a record speed of 320 mph (515 kph).
•**1990** The city of Los Angeles, where 3 million people go to work daily by car, finally opens a commuter rail system.

•**1991** Work on a commercial maglev railroad starts in Florida.
•**1992** The Japanese *Yamoto 1* is the first ship to be propelled by magnetic forces.
•**1992** Japan is now the world's leading shipbuilding country.
•**1993** Engineers in Europe and America develop ideas for a successor to the Concorde.
•**1993** Russia and America agree to work on a permanent orbiting space station.

Impact electric car, 1990

•**1993** In preparation for possible future exploration of Mars, an eight-legged robot called *Dante* walks into the mouth of an active volcano in Antarctica.
•**1993** New laws in California say that 10 percent of cars sold there after 2003 must be emission-free.
•**1993** The robot space probe *Pioneer 10*, launched from the US in 1972, is now 5 billion miles (8 billion kilometers) from Earth.
1994 The world's largest hovercraft, *Hisho* (meaning "Flight"), is launched.

Channel Tunnel train, 1994

•**1994** The rail link between England and France through the 30-mile (50-km) Channel Tunnel officially opens.
•**1994** Cable-stayed bridges (supported by slanting cables attached to a single tower) are coming into use.
•**1994** Work begins on a scheme to create an artificial island in Hong Kong harbor, on which the world's biggest airport will be built.
•**1994** A solar-powered car, *Aurora Q1*, crosses Australia in 8 days, averaging 30 mph (50 kph).

Future trends

Design for a future supersonic airliner

SUPERSONIC AIRLINERS

To meet the demand for rapid business travel, a new generation of supersonic airliners is being planned. These aircraft will be quieter than the Concorde and able to carry twice as many passengers over distances of up to 8,000 miles (13,000 km). The costs will be so high that only an international consortium of companies will be able to afford to develop such an aircraft. Major airlines may prefer to see a new series of economical "superjumbo" jets, able to carry more passengers than ever before.

SPACE STATION

There are still plans to build a permanent space station that would enable scientists in space to carry out experiments and study the Earth and the stars. It would also make it much simpler to repair damaged satellites because engineers would travel from the space station rather than from Earth.

With wings folded, HL-20 fits in space shuttle.

Full-scale model of the HL-20

Andromeda Galaxy

Space station

SPACE TAXIS

If permanent space stations become a reality, small, economical space vehicles will be needed to ferry crews to and from the Earth. One such vehicle under development is the HL-20, a sort of scaled-down version of the space shuttle. Launched by an expendable booster, it would use its wings to make a normal runway landing. With its wings folded, this versatile craft would be small enough to be carried in the cargo bay of the main space shuttle if necessary.

INTERSTELLAR TRAVEL

Unfortunately, the galaxies, stars, and planets beyond our Solar System are so far away that it is doubtful whether we will ever be able to send astronauts to them. For example, the nearest star to the Earth is 4.2 light-years away. It is more likely that we will explore the Universe using robot spacecraft that will relay information back to Earth.

Experimental high-mileage cars

THE FUTURE OF THE CAR

Faced with dwindling energy supplies, the cars of the future will have to use less fuel and cause less pollution. This could be achieved by using lightweight materials, such as carbon-fiber and aluminum, to make smaller cars that will get more miles to the gallon of gasoline. Electric cars are only a partial solution because fossil fuels still have to be burned in power stations to make electricity to recharge the cars' batteries. Solar-powered cars may one day become viable in warm climates.

MORE POWER, MORE SPEED

Our obsession with speed shows no sign of waning. Record breakers such as Craig Breedlove and Richard Noble (*see* **MILESTONES 1965** *and* **1983**) aim to build supersonic cars that will reach speeds of 745 mph (1,200 kph) or more. Although some people consider this very wasteful, the lessons learned from such cars help designers develop better cars for everyday use.

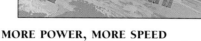

New streetcar system in Manchester, England

STREETCARS REBORN

As city centers around the world become choked with traffic, many city authorities are building rapid-transit systems to lure people away from their cars and to free the streets of congestion. Underground railroads continue to play a vital role, but there are many new light railroads being built, and in some cities streetcars are being reintroduced decades after they were withdrawn.

Richard Noble's *Thrust SSC* supersonic car

AN END TO COMMUTING?

One of the main reasons that people travel into city centers is to get to work. But changing work patterns may also change the face of city travel. Many more people are now working from home on computers, and using telephones, modems, and fax machines to communicate with their employers. Crowded commuter trains and buses, long delays, and traffic jams may one day be a thing of the past.

Working from home

SUPERCRUISERS

The enduring popularity of sea cruises has prompted cruise lines to plan new, ever-larger cruise ships exceeding 110,000 tons (100,000 tonnes). These "supercruisers" will offer all the usual luxuries, as well as high-tech facilities such as virtual reality theater and retractable domes to cover on-deck swimming pools in bad weather.

This 110,000-ton (100,000-tonne) cruiser will be the biggest passenger ship ever built

NEW HULL DESIGNS

The future of fast sea transportation may lie with SWATH (Small Water Area Twin Hull) vessels, which look like a cross between a catamaran and a hydrofoil. A SWATH vessel floats on two long pods below the waterline. The rest of the ship stands clear of the water on slim struts. Only the struts cut through the waves, enabling the ship to ride rough seas at high speeds using less power than ships with normal hulls.

Experimental Russian WIG

WING-IN-GROUND EFFECT CRAFT

Jet airliners experience the "ground effect" as they land. A cushion of air trapped between the wings and the runway causes extra lift. "Wing-in-ground effect" watercraft (or WIGs) use this phenomenon to skim across the water on a cushion of air like a hovercraft – but they can travel much faster. WIGs are still in the developmental stage, but may one day provide rapid transportation across lakes and between coastal islands.

Artist's impression of the "Super Technoliner" SWATH cargo ship under development in Japan

Index

Emergency ambulance, 1990s

"Deltic" Diesel-Electric Locomotive, 1956

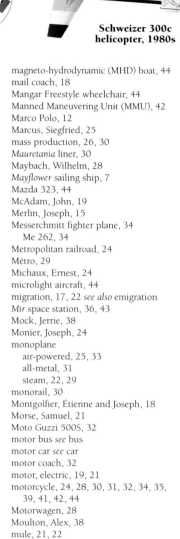

Schweizer 300c helicopter, 1980s

Battery-powered car for disabled drivers, 1990s

Acknowledgments

Dorling Kindersley would like to thank:
The staff of the National Maritime Museum and the Science Museum; Esther Labi for editorial assistance; Robin Hunter and Kate Eagar for design help; Sarah Hill; British Museum Education Service; Museum of Mankind; Royal Institute of Natural Architects.

Key: l=left r= right c=center t=top b=bottom or below a=above

Special Photography: Tina Chambers for photography at National Maritime Museum. David Exton and John Lepine for photography at the Science Museum.
Additional Photography: American Museum of Natural History (artefact 50/5756); Ashmolean Museum; British Library; British Museum; ESA; Exeter Maritime Museum; London Planetarium; Museum of Mankind/British Museum; National Maritime Museum; National Motor Museum, Beaulieu; National Railway Museum, York; Noordwijk Space Expo; The Royal Armouries, Royal Artillery Trust, Woolwich; Science Museum.
Photographers: Peter Anderson; Geoff Brightling; Martin Cameron; Peter Chadwick; Andy Crawford; Geoff Downs; Peter Downs; Mike Dunning; Lynton Gardiner; Philip Gatward; Christi Graham; Peter Hayman; Dudley Hubbard; Dave King; Richard Leeney; Ray Moller; Nick Nicholls; Susanna Price; James Stevenson; Clive Streeter; Matthew Ward; Jerry Young.
Illustrators: David Ashby 10cr; Russell Barnett 9tr, 9br, 12tl; Luciano Corbello 42tl, 42bl; David Pugh, 41t.
Picture Credits: Lesley & Roy Adkins 7crb; Advertising Archives 33cla; J.A. Allen & Co. Ltd/Major A.B. Shone 14cla; Archiv für Kunst und Geschichte 10bc, 26clb, 28br, 31bc, 33bc/Musée du Louvre 10tc
Arcwind Ltd 41cb; Ashmolean Museum, Oxford 9tc; Australian High Commission, London 40cl; Aviation Photographs International 34tl, 41tr, 43tr, 45tl; Aviation Picture Library/Austin Brown 33tc, 43tcb;; Stephen Piercey 34ca; Avico Press/Aleksander Belyaev 45bl; Photos courtesy of The Boeing Company 40tl, 41clb; Bridgeman Art Library/National Railway Museum, York 17bl; British Library; British Museum 6tl; Neill Bruce/ Peter Roberts Collection 26tr; Peter A. Clayton 6bla; Coo-ee Historical; Picture Library 32tr; Culver Pictures 19c; Devonshire Collection, Chatsworth. Reproduced by permission of the Chatsworth Settlement

Trustees 14cr; C.M. Dixon 6tr; ET Archive 6bra, 7bc, 14tr, 18cra, 21cla/Bibliotheque Nationale; Paris 12cr; British Museum 9c; Ironbridge Gorge Museum 17crb; Mary Evans 8tr, 8cr, 8crb, 11cra, 13tc, 13br, 14ca, 15tc, 15tr, 16tr, 16bc, 18tr, 20bc, 21cb, 22c, 23tc, 23bc, 24cr, 25bc, 27tl, 27bl, 27crb, 28clb, 28tr, 29ca, 29br, 30tl, 31cr, 32tc, 34bc; Werner Forman Archive/Nick Saunders 13tcr; Genesis Space Photo Library 35br, 37tr; Robert; Harding/Nelly Boyd 45cra; Wilbur House, Hull City Museum & Art Galleries 16crb; Hulton Deutsch Collection 15cb, 18clb, 24tr, 35bl, 39bc, 40br; Images Colour Library 43cb; Image Select 26tl; Imperial War Museum 34c; London Transport Museum 24cl, 30cla, 31cra, 32cla; Maclaren 39cl; Master & Fellows, Magdalene College, Cambridge 13c; Magnum/Rene Burri 43tl; Jean Gaumy 38cb; Mangar Aids Ltd 44cl; Mansell Collection 22tl, 23tl, 24crb, 25cb; Mercedes Benz 32cl, 36bc; Musée J.Armand Bombardier, Québec 34bl; NASA 40tr, 40tcb, 42tc, 42tr, 45tcr, 45tcl/JPL 36tc; National Maritime Museum 14bc; National Motor Museum, Beaulieu 38cra; National Museums of Scotland/Scottish Ethnological Archive 27clb; Peter Newark's Pictures 17cb, 24bc, 28cl, 30bc, 33c, 34cl, 34clb, 35cra, 35c; Nissan 41bc; Novosti 38bc; Robert Opie Collection 26br, 28bl; Pictor International 37crb, 42br; Pitt Rivers Museum 22-23c; Popperfoto 37bc; Rex Features 42cl; Ann Ronan at Image Select 16br, 19tr, 21cl; Royal Aeronautical Society 20tl, 24tl, 31tc, 33tr; Royal Navy Submarine Museum 15br; Science Museum/Science & Society Picture Library 3bl, 8tl, 17tc, 18cl, 19crb, 21c, 21br, 23ct, 23tr, 23crb, 25tl, 27cl, 28tl, 29tc, 29cr, 35bra; Science Photo Library/Martin Bond 36bc; Tony Hallas 45tr; NASA 32bc; Sea Containers 44clb, 44cbl; Frank Spooner Pictures 43br, 44bl/Alain le Bot 45cl; Mitsuhiro Wada 44cb;Tony Stone Images 38cr/Warren Jacobs 43cra; Martin Rogers 41crb Technological Research Association of Techno-Superliner, Tokyo 45br; Transport Know How Ltd 41c; TRH/DOD 34cla; Westland 35bla; Triumph Motorcycles Ltd 44cr; Michael Turner 45c; University Museum of National Antiquities Oslo, Norway 11br; Westland Group 44tr; Noel Whittall 41tl; York Archaeological Trust 11bc.

East Indiaman, 17th century